PowerBASIC Explained

OTHER TITLES OF INTEREST

BP313	A Concise Introduction To Sage
BP323	How To Choose a Small Business Computer System
BP328	Sage Explained
BP360	A Practical Introduction to Sage Sterling +2 for Windows
BP361	Sage Sterling +2 for Windows Explained
BP389	PowerPoint for Windows Explained
BP398	Sage Instant Accounting Explained
BP417	Explaining Microsoft Publisher for Windows 95
BP440	Explaining Microsoft Money 97
BP441	Creating Web Pages using Microsoft Office 97
BP442	Explaining Microsoft Publisher 97

PowerPoint 97 Explained

by

David Weale

BERNARD BABANI (publishing) LTD
THE GRAMPIANS
SHEPHERDS BUSH ROAD
LONDON W6 7NF
ENGLAND

PLEASE NOTE

Although every care has been taken with the production of this book to ensure that any instructions or any of the other contents operate in a correct and safe manner, the Author and the Publishers do not accept any responsibility for any failure, damage or loss caused by following the said contents. The Author and Publisher do not take any responsibility for errors or omissions.

The Author and Publisher will not be liable to the purchaser or to any other person or legal entity with respect to any liability, loss or damage (whether direct, indirect, special, incidental or consequential) caused or alleged to be caused directly or indirectly by this book.

The book is sold as is, without any warranty of any kind, either expressed or implied, respecting the contents, including but not limited to implied warranties regarding the book's quality, performance, correctness or fitness for any particular purpose.

No part of this book may be reproduced or copied by any means whatever without written permission of the Publisher.

All rights reserved

© 1998 BERNARD BABANI (publishing) LTD
Screen Shot(s) reprinted with permission from Microsoft Corporation.
First published - April 1998
British Library Cataloguing in Publication Data
A catalogue record for this work is available from the British Library
ISBN 0 85934 443 6

Cover design by Gregor Arthur
Cover illustration by Adam Willis
Printed and bound in Great Britain by Cox & Wyman Ltd., Reading.

Preface

Welcome to this book, I wrote it to explain the program in a way that looks at how to actually produce and enhance your own presentations.

I have used PowerPoint to create my own slide shows and presentations for some years and it is an excellent program. The latest version contains all the strengths of the previous versions together with some super additional features, including the creation of Web (Internet) pages

Each chapter of the book covers an aspect of the program and contains various hints and techniques that may not be obvious.

The text has been written both with the new user in mind and for the experienced person as it contains explanations of the more technical and sophisticated features

You should understand the basic techniques of using Windows 95 itself. If you do not then there are many excellent texts on the market.

I hope you learn from this book and have as much enjoyment using the program as I do.

David Weale, April 1998

ABOUT THE AUTHOR

David Weale is a Fellow of the Institute of Chartered Accountants and has worked in both private and public practice. He is a lecturer in business computing at Yeovil College.

He is the author of several books on computing and lives in Somerset with his wife, three children and two Siamese cats.

DEDICATION

To my father.

x

TRADEMARKS

PowerPoint is a registered trademark of Microsoft Corporation.

Microsoft®, Microsoft® Windows® and Wingdings® are also registered trademarks of Microsoft Corporation.

All other trademarks are the registered and legally protected trademarks of the companies who make the products. There is no intent to use the trademarks generally and readers should investigate ownership of a trademark before using it for any purpose.

Contents

BEGINNINGS 1
   The Pull Down Menus 1
   The Toolbars 2

Creating a presentation 2

AutoContent Wizard 3
   Viewing the slides 6

Template 8
   Altering the Layout 10
   Altering the Design 11

Blank Presentation 12

Opening a presentation 14

LOOKING AT YOUR SLIDES 15

Slide View 16

Outline View 17

Slide Sorter View 20

Notes Page View 22

Slide Show 22

OUTPUT 23

Slide Shows 24
- The Slide Show menu 25
- Next/Previous/Go.. 25
- Custom Show 26
- Meeting Minder 27
- Speaker Notes 28
- Slide Meter... 28
- Arrow/Pen/Pointer Options................................ 29
- Screen/End Show 29

Printing onto Paper 30

SAVING YOUR WORK 32

TEXT 34

Entering Text 34
- Altering the Font 36

Spell Checking Your Text 38

ADDING GRAPHICS & OBJECTS 39

Clipart 40
- Adding pictures, sounds and videos................... 41

A Word for Windows Table 42

Graphs.. 44

WordArt.. 48

- Organisation Charts 51
  - File Menu 52
  - Edit 52
  - View 53
  - Styles 53
  - Text 54
  - Boxes 55
  - Lines 55
  - Chart 55
  - Help 55
  - Toolbar Buttons 56
- Other Objects 57

ARTWORK 58

- Manipulating Images 58
  - Moving an Image or Other Object 58
  - Sizing an Image or Object 58
  - Cropping an Object 60

ALTERING YOUR SLIDES 63
- Making Changes to the Master Slide 63
- Deleting Slides 64

  Drawing toolbar 65
   Draw 66
   Grouping and Ungrouping 66
   Superimposing One Image on Another 68
   Order 70
   Bring to Front 70
   Send to Back 70
   Bring Forward 70
   Send Backward 70
   Snap 71
   Nudge 71
   Align or Distribute 71
   Rotate or Flip 72
   Rotating Text 73
   Edit Points 73
   Change AutoShape 73
   AutoShapes and other shapes 74
   WordArt 75

CREATING WEB PAGES 76
  Existing presentations 76
  Online designs 76
  Saving a PowerPoint file as HTML 78
  Banners 86

THE PULL DOWN MENUS 88

File menu 88
- Pack and Go 89
- Send To 92
- Mail Recipient 92
- Routing Recipient 93
- Exchange Folder 94
- Microsoft Word 95
- Properties 96

Edit menu 98
- Cut, Copy and Paste 98
- Paste Special 99
- Paste as Hyperlink 99
- Clear 99
- Select All 99
- Duplicate 100
- Delete Slide 100
- Find 101
- Replace 101
- Go to Property 102
- Links 104
- Objects 104

View menu 105
- Black and White 105
- Slide Miniature 105
- Toolbars 106
- Rulers 107
- Guides 107
- Headers and Footers 108
- Comments 110

Insert menu 111
  Duplicate Slide... 111
  Slide Number / Date and Time 112
  Tab 112
  Comment... 113
  Slides from Files 114
  Slides from Outline 114
  Pictures 115
  Text Box 117
  Movies and Sounds 117

Format menu... 121
  Font.. 122
  Changing the Bullets... 123
  Alignment 124
  Line Spacing 124
  Change Case 126
  Replacing Fonts 127
  Slide Colour Scheme 128
  Background... 130
  Colour and Lines.. 130
  Object / Picture 132
  Format Painter 134

Tools menu 135
　Style Checker 136
　Language 137
　AutoCorrect 138
　Look Up Reference 139
　AutoClipArt 140
　PowerPoint Central 141
　Presentation Conference 142
　Expand Slide 142
　Macro 142
　Add-Ins 142
　Customise 143
　Options 145

Slide Show Menu 147
　View Show 147
　Rehearse Timings 148
　Record Narration 149
　Set Up Show 150
　View On Two Screens 151
　Action Buttons 152
　Action Settings 156
　Preset Animation 157
　Custom Animation 158
　Animation Preview 159
　Slide Transition 160
　Hide Slide 161
　Displaying Hidden Slides 161
　Custom Shows 162
　Jumping to other slide shows 162

THE HELP MENU 163
Contents and Index 163
Contents 164
Index 167
Find 168
The Office Assistant 171
What's This? 171
Microsoft on the Web 172
About Microsoft PowerPoint 174

COPING WITH PRESENTATIONS 176
First Things 176
The Material 176
The Presentation 177
The Environment Itself 178
Using Software 178
Layout 179
Colours and Things 180

Beginnings

When you load Microsoft® PowerPoint, you will see the screen shown below.

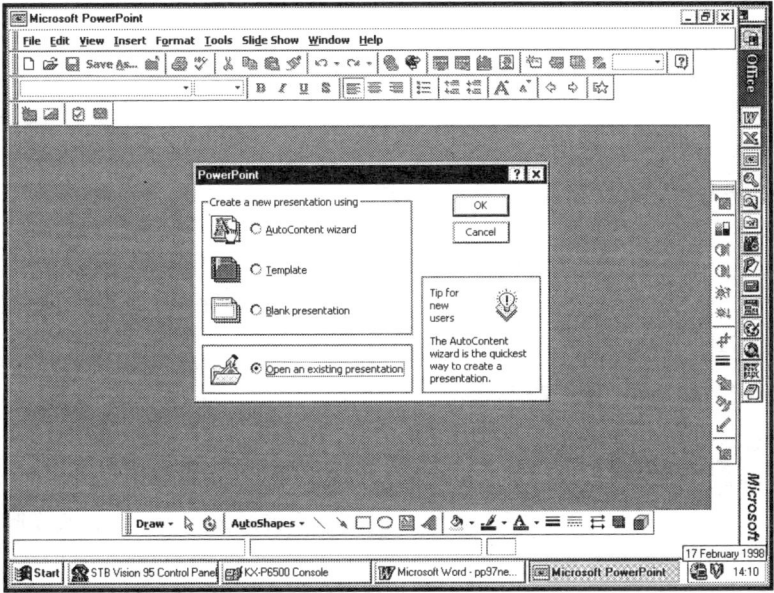

The Pull Down Menus

Along the top of the screen are the pull down menus. When you click the (left) mouse button on any of these, a pull down menu will appear. Each contains several related commands (some of which can also be carried out using the toolbar buttons).

The Toolbars

Along the top of the screen are two toolbars, these contain buttons which you can click on to carry out activities or commands.

The toolbar buttons are a quicker alternative to using the pull down menus and you can add or remove buttons as you wish to reflect your own especial methods or requirements (**Tools, Customise**).

If you position the mouse pointer over any of the buttons, a description will appear.

If you click the right hand mouse button while pointing at any button a pull down menu will appear with various commands.

Creating a presentation

As you can see from the previous screen, you are given four choices:

☐ AutoContent wizard

☐ Template

☐ Blank presentation

☐ Open an existing presentation

We will look at each in turn.

AutoContent Wizard

This guides you through a series of steps. You enter various details or make choices in each. The result is a professional presentation that you have created in a very short time.

The first screen is shown below.

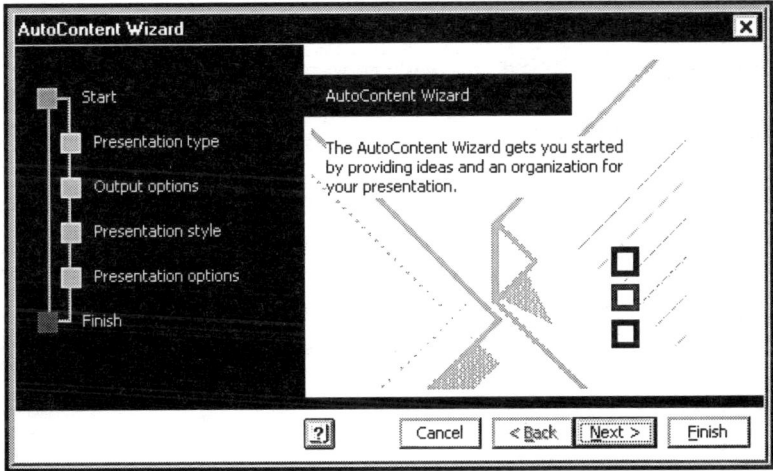

This is followed by a series of other screens, the content of which will differ depending upon your choices.

As you can see from the next screen, there are a variety of different presentation wizards to choose from (including web page presentations that can be put onto the Internet or your organisation's Intranet).

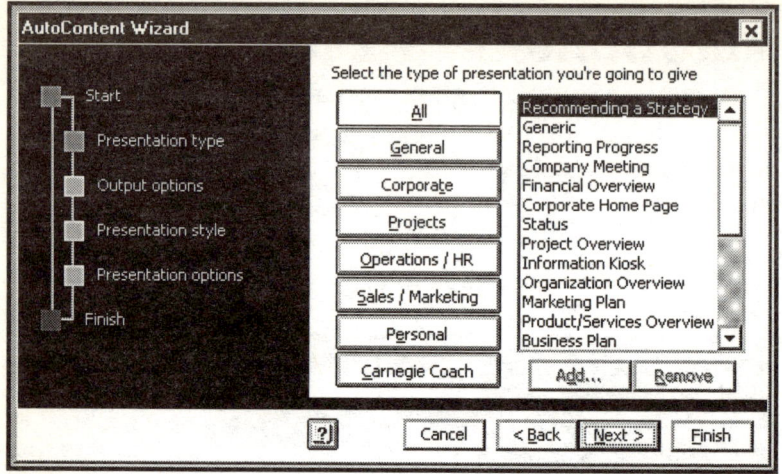

When you have finished, the Wizard leaves you with an Outline of the presentation with prompting text already in place. All you have to do is to alter the text (by highlighting and overwriting) to whatever you wish to say. You can add or delete slides as you wish.

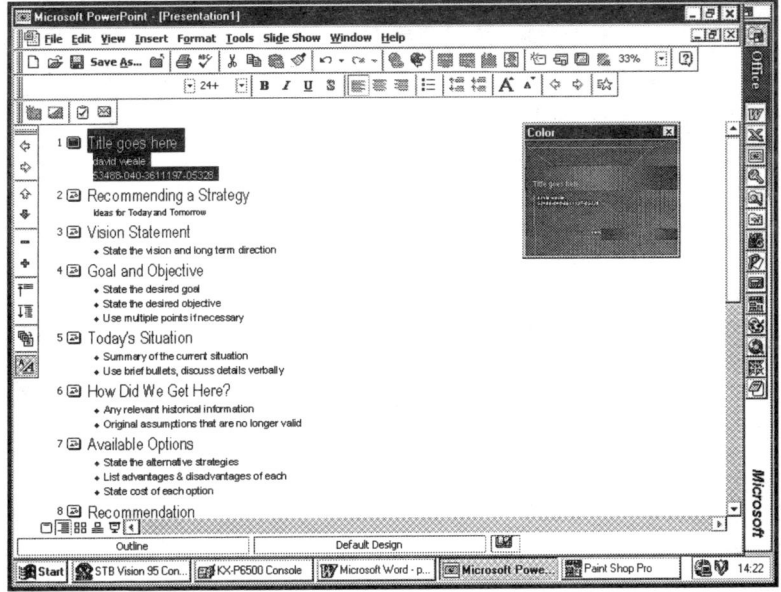

Viewing the slides

When you have finished creating the slide show, you can look at all the slides by clicking on the **Slide Sorter View** button (along the bottom of the screen).

You will see the following display.

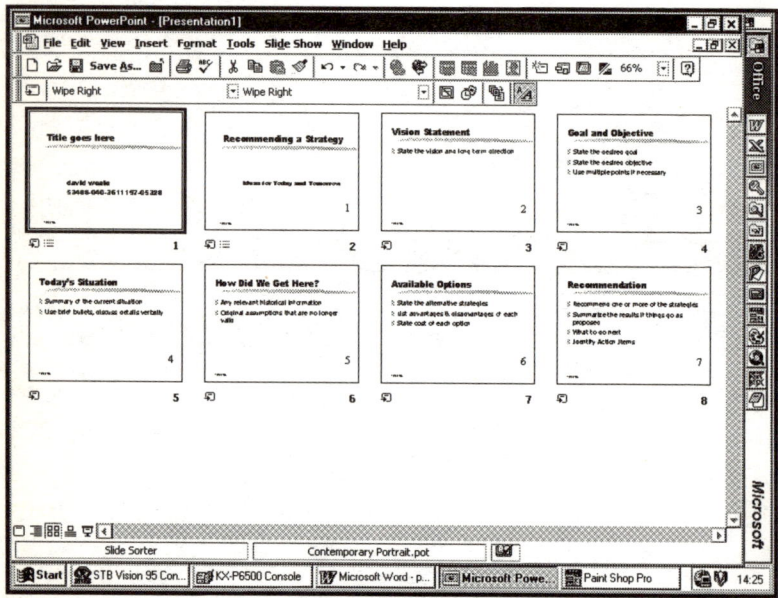

If you want to look at each slide in turn then you need to click on the **Slide View** button (again along the bottom of the screen) to make the slides full screen.

The initial slide may look similar to this.

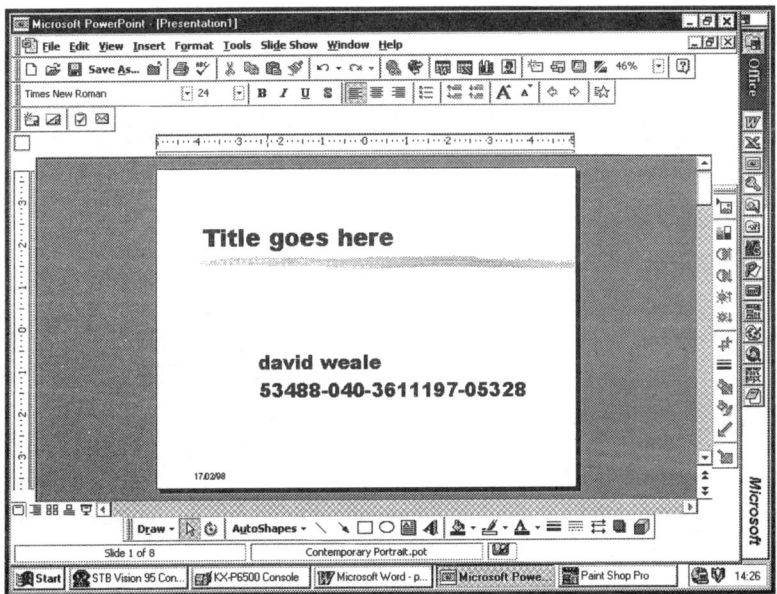

You can move from slide to slide by clicking on the double-arrowhead buttons (on the bottom right of the screen)

You can view the slide show as it would appear on an OHP or projected onto a screen by clicking on the **Show** button along the bottom of the screen.

Template

The second option when starting a presentation is the template. After selecting this, you will see the following.

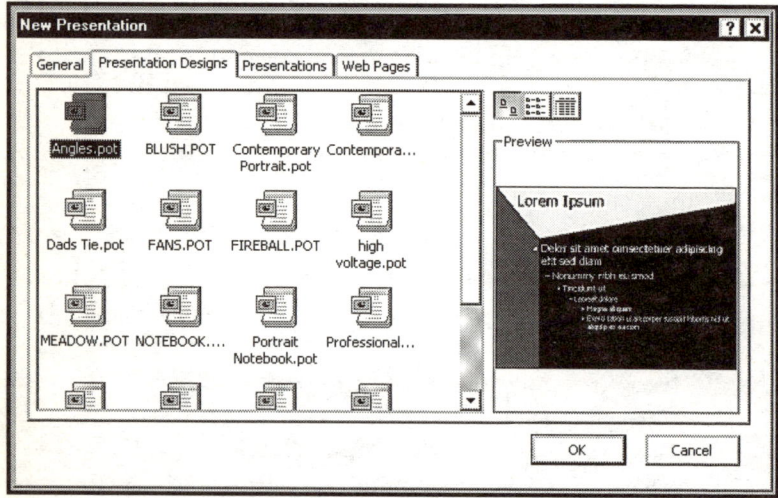

You can look at the display in three different ways as **Large Icons**, **List** or **Details**. To alter the display click on the appropriate button (to the right of the dialog box).

When you select one of the designs, a small preview is shown on the right.

After you have chosen your design and clicked on the **OK** button, you will be asked to select a **Layout**. The title layout is the default.

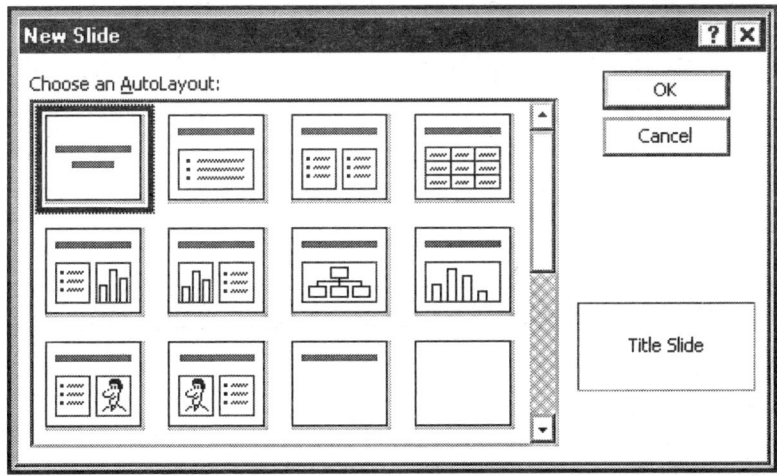

Finally you will see the slide; you then add your own text to replace the existing text by clicking and typing.

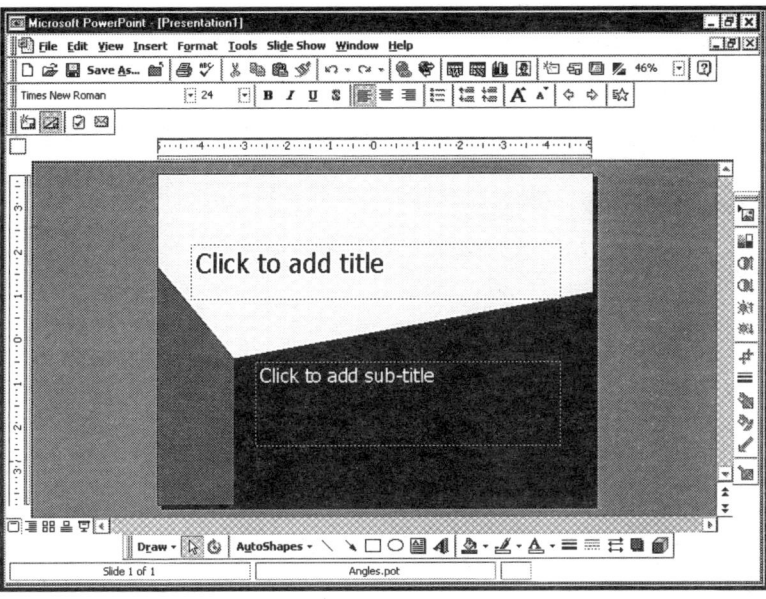

Altering the Layout

To alter the layout, click on the **Slide Layout** button (upper toolbar) and select an alternative layout. This is slightly different to the original layout screen as it allows you to **Reapply** a layout.

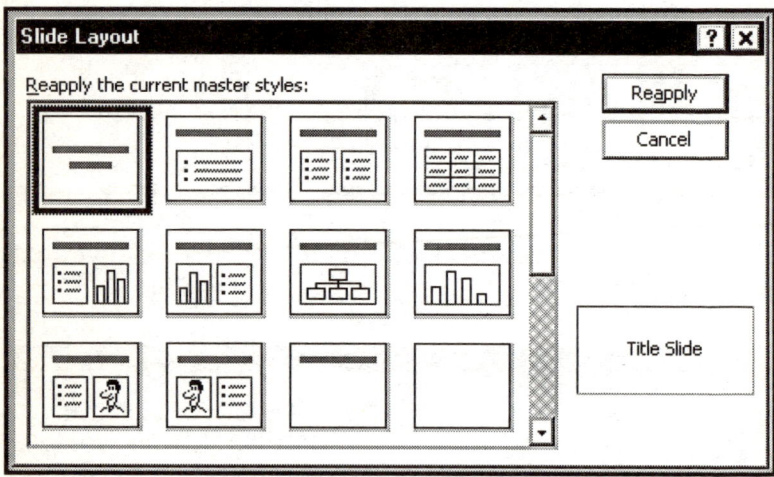

Altering the Design

You can click on the **Apply Design** button (upper toolbar) to alter the design. This lets you alter a design at any time.

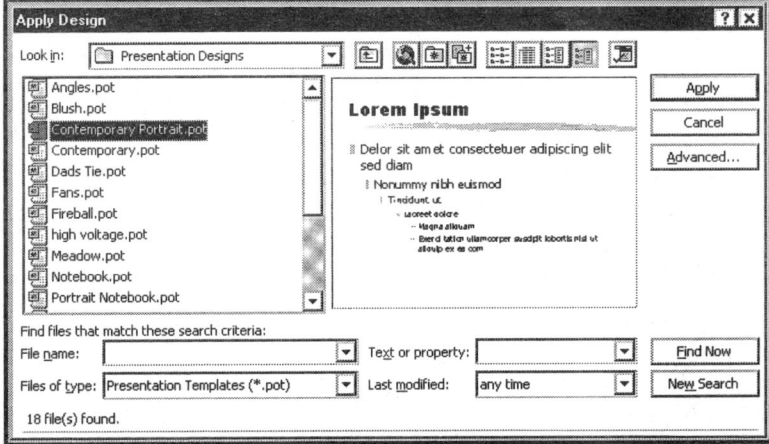

Be careful to apply the design early on, if you alter the fonts or layout of a slide show and **then** alter the design, the new design imposes its own formatting on the slides, e.g. fonts and colour scheme.

Blank Presentation

The third choice of new presentation is the blank presentation. This gives you a choice of layout without the addition of a design. The only dialog box is shown below.

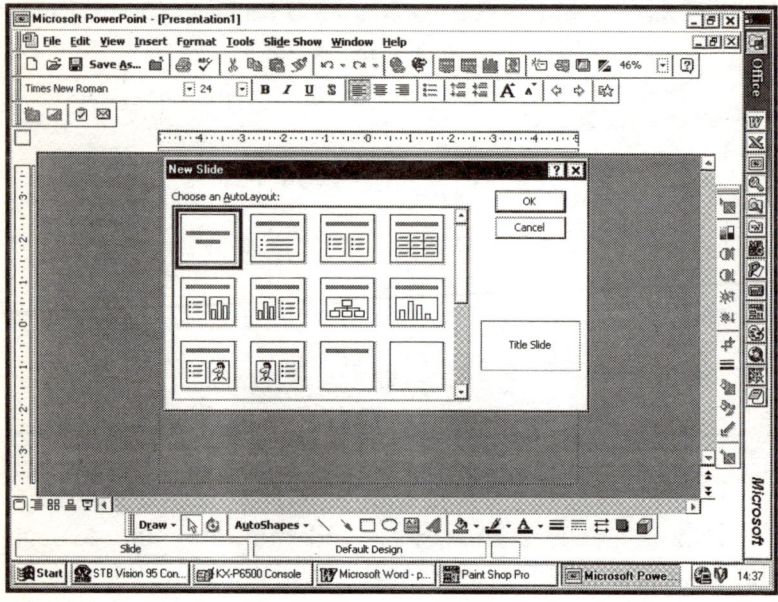

This is an ideal choice if you wish to apply a design at a later stage.

A blank presentation looks like this.

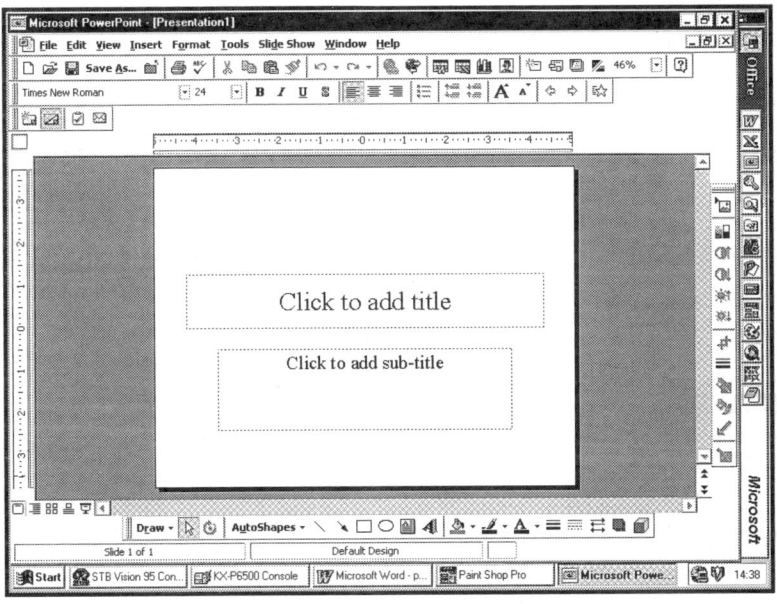

Opening a presentation

Selecting this option displays the **Open** dialog box. You need to find the file you wish to open.

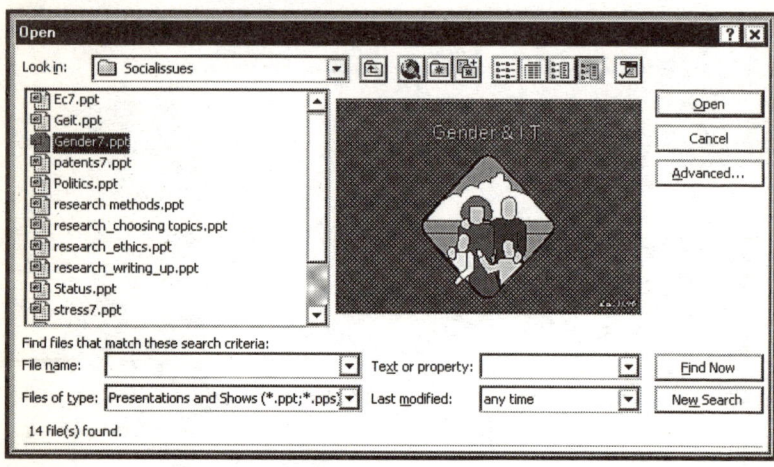

Looking at Your Slides

There are several ways of looking at the slides. You can access these from the **View** menu or from the buttons along the bottom left of the screen.

- ☐ Slide View

- ☐ Outline View

- ☐ Slide Sorter View

- ☐ Notes Page View

- ☐ Slide Show

Slide View

This is the default (the normal way the slides are displayed). Each slide is shown full screen and you can move from slide to slide by using the buttons on the right of the screen.

You can alter the size of the display either by clicking on the **Zoom Control** button on the upper toolbar, or by pulling down the **View** menu and choosing **Zoom**. This gives more control as you can enter a figure.

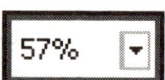

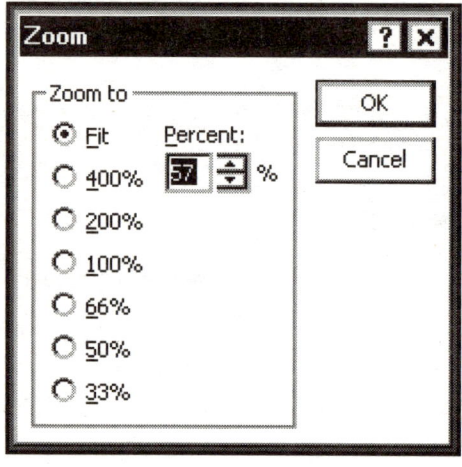

Outline View

Only the titles and main text of all your slides are shown, each slide is numbered and they are shown in sequence.

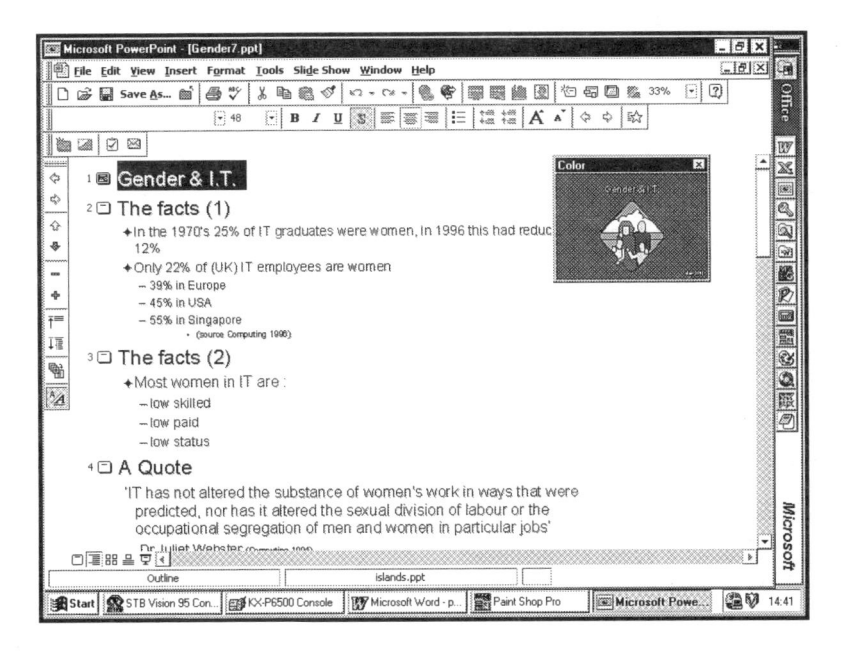

Outline has two major uses:

☐ Being able to see all the main text in this way lets you alter the formatting and rearrange it more easily.

☐ You can import outlines from other programs, such as Word by selecting the **File** menu, clicking on **Open** and in the **Files of type** box, click **All Outlines**. In the **Name** box, double-click the document you want to use.

The screen below shows an example of this technique.

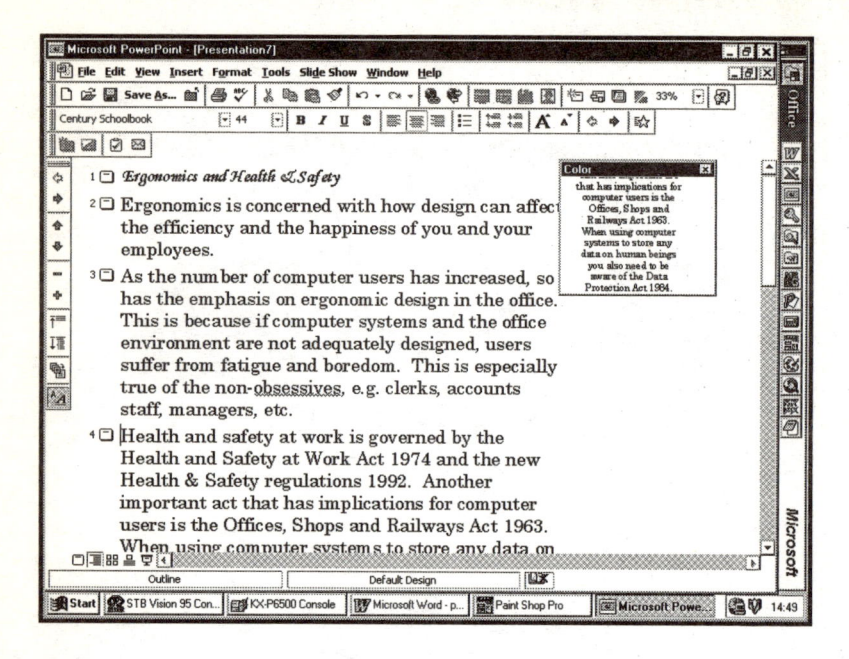

Note that you can import from web (HTML files) as well as more traditional file types.

The buttons specific to outlines are described here.

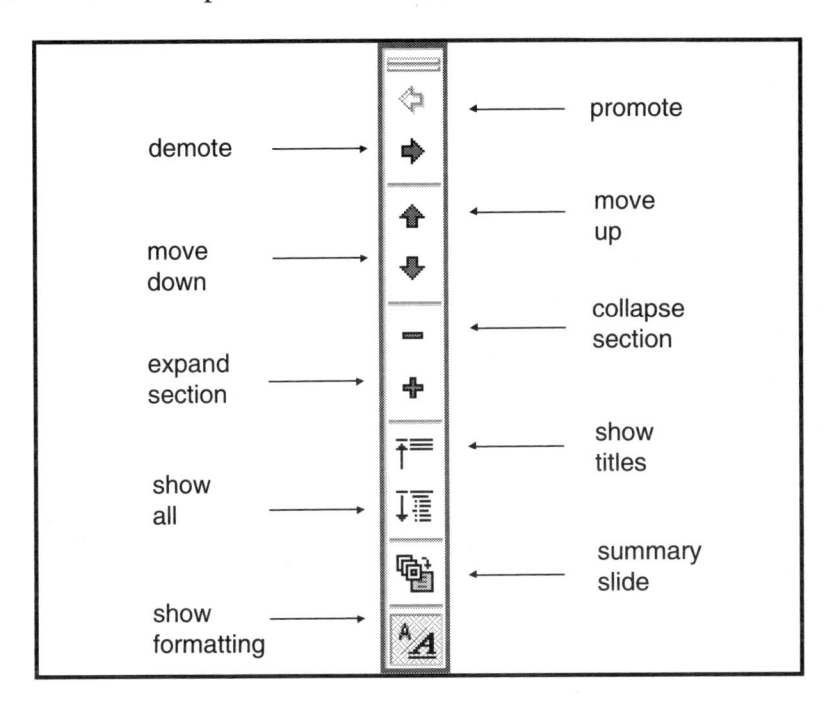

Label (left)		Label (right)
		promote
demote		
		move up
move down		
		collapse section
expand section		
		show titles
show all		
		summary slide
show formatting		

You can use the **Tab** key to move a line down a level or use **Shift** and **Tab** to move it up instead of the buttons.

Slide Sorter View

Using this lets you display (small) images of all your slides in sequence. Using this feature lets you:

☐ Rearrange the sequence.

Or

☐ **Select All** from the **Edit** menu and apply special effects such as **Transitions** and **Animations** to all the slides.

The screen looks like this:

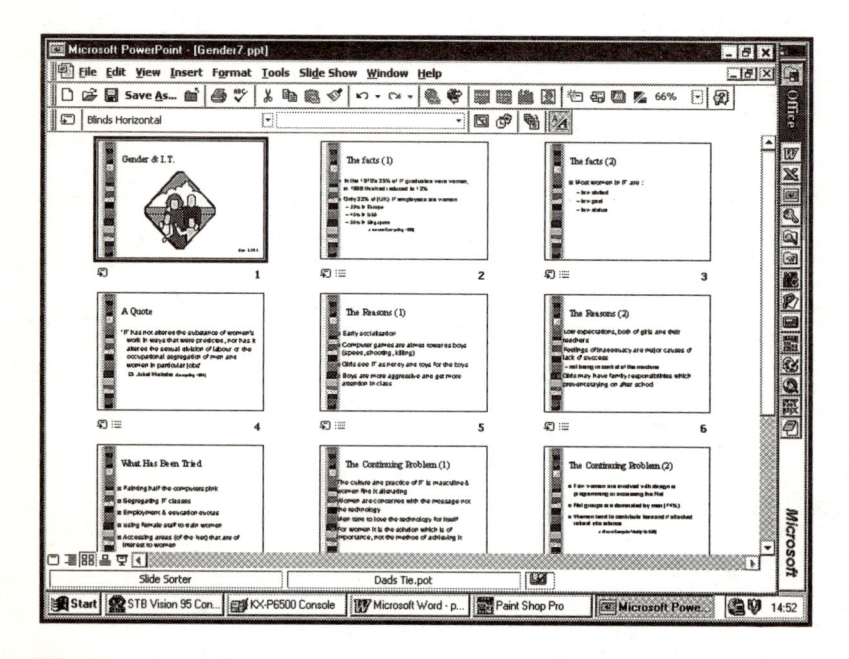

To alter the size of the slides use the **Zoom** button.

To move the slides around, simply click on a slide with the mouse and then drag it to a new position (between two slides). The other slides will rearrange themselves.

Notes Page View

Useful for the person who is actually doing the presentation. This lets you add text notes to a page that contains a slide in the top half.

The screen looks like this:

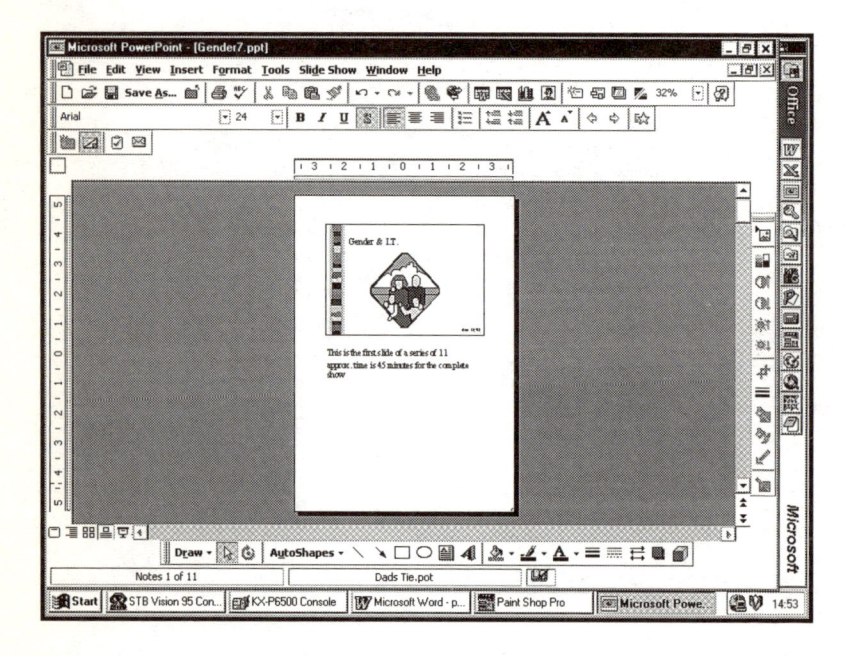

You add your own text, comments and so on in the space in the bottom half of the page. Each slide is allocated its own page for notes

Slide Show

This is dealt with in the next section on **Output**.

Output

You can output your presentation slides in various ways.

☐ As a slide show either on the computer screen or using a LCD panel and an overhead projector (OHP) onto a wall screen.

☐ Output it to a floppy disc for use with a computer that does not have the PowerPoint viewer installed on it (this is legal).

☐ Print to paper as individual slides, speaker notes, and handouts or in outline form.

☐ Print directly onto OHP film (in either B&W or colour).

Slide Shows

This is the most effective way of presenting and you can build in special effects such as **Transitions** and **Animations**.

Make sure you are at the start of the slides and then click on the **Slide Show** button along the bottom of the screen.

Your slides will then appear one after the other on the screen.

To advance to the next slide click the left-hand mouse button.

The Slide Show menu

If you click the **right hand** mouse button during a slide show, the following menu is displayed.

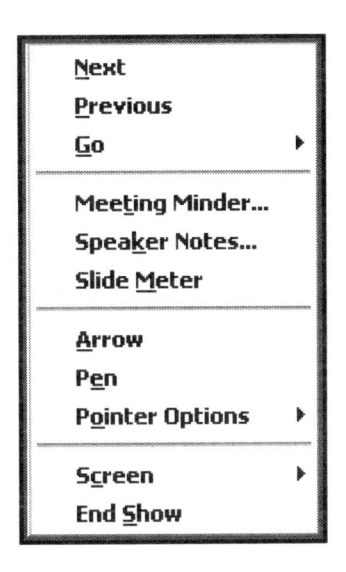

```
Next
Previous
Go                    ▶
─────────────────────
Meeting Minder...
Speaker Notes...
Slide Meter
─────────────────────
Arrow
Pen
Pointer Options      ▶
─────────────────────
Screen               ▶
End Show
```

Most of these are explained as they are fundamental to your slide show.

Next/Previous/Go

To move to the next or previous point. The Go option has a sub menu.

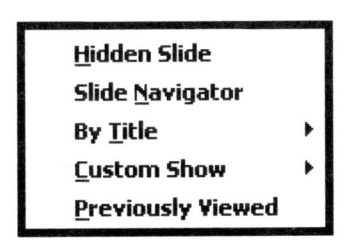

```
Hidden Slide
Slide Navigator
By Title             ▶
Custom Show          ▶
Previously Viewed
```

Hidden Slide
This will display a hidden slide (you have to be viewing the slide before a hidden slide for this to be available).

Slide Navigator/By Title
Selecting one of these displays a list of slides (Navigator) or titles (Title), if you choose one of these then the corresponding slide will be displayed. The Navigator menu is shown for reference.

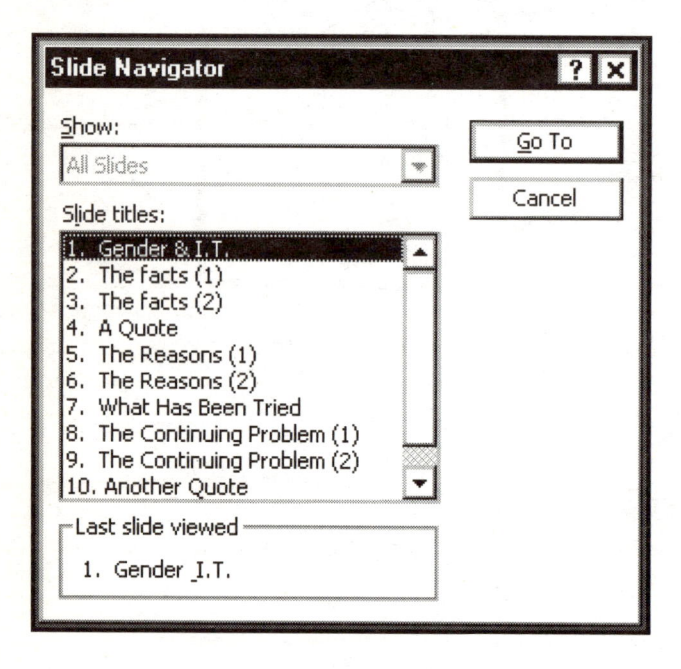

Custom Show
This jumps to a custom show (you have to have created a custom show - **Slide Show** and **Custom Shows**).

Meeting Minder

You can add notes or minutes during the presentation by selecting this option. Only you will see the display.

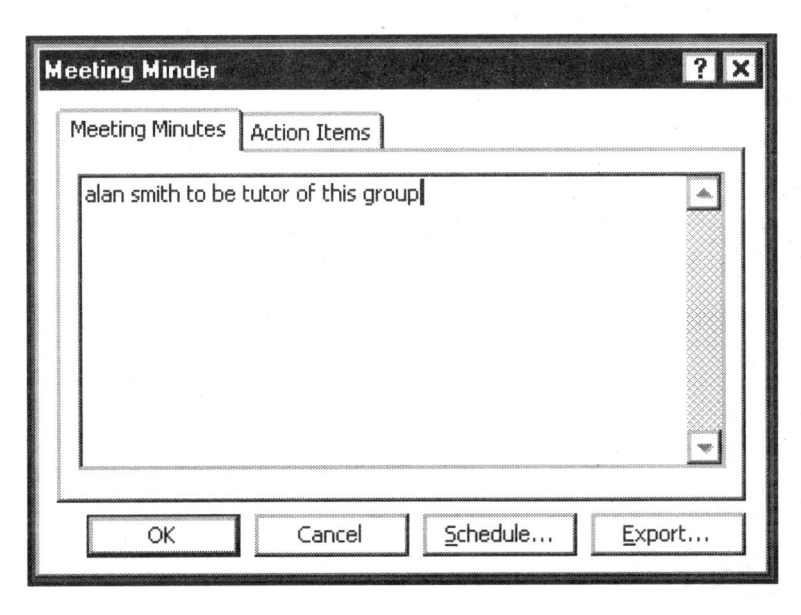

If you have **Word** or **Outlook** installed you can **Export** or **Schedule** the text.

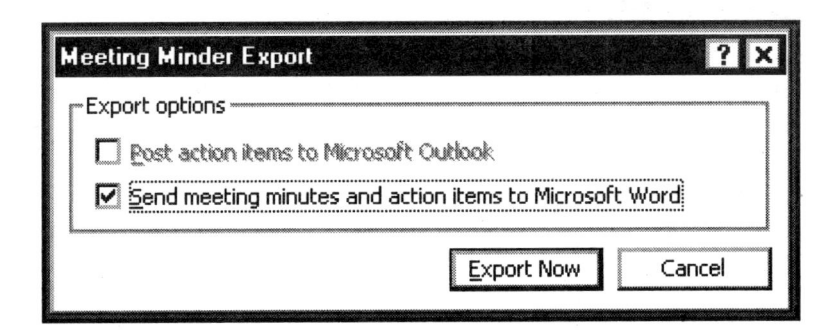

Speaker Notes

If you have created speaker notes, these can be displayed on your screen.

Slide Meter

If you have set automatic timings for your slide show but then choose to advance the slides manually, you can check your progress against the timings you set.

Arrow/Pen/Pointer Options

You can change the arrow to a pen so that you can write on the screen (whether this is legible depends upon your mouse control). You can hide the pointer so that it never appears and you can alter the colour of the pen.

Screen/End Show

You can **Pause** the screen (when using automatic timings), **Black** the screen and if you have used the pen, you can **Erase** the pen (your writing).

I suggest you end the slide show either with a black screen or have a final slide that you can leave while you answer questions, for example your company logo. This is more professional than just ending the show.

You can also choose to **End Show**, which ends it abruptly.

Printing onto Paper

To print your file click on the **Print** button along the upper toolbar.

However, if you pull down the **File** menu and select **Print** you will see the following dialog box that offers you a variety of choices.

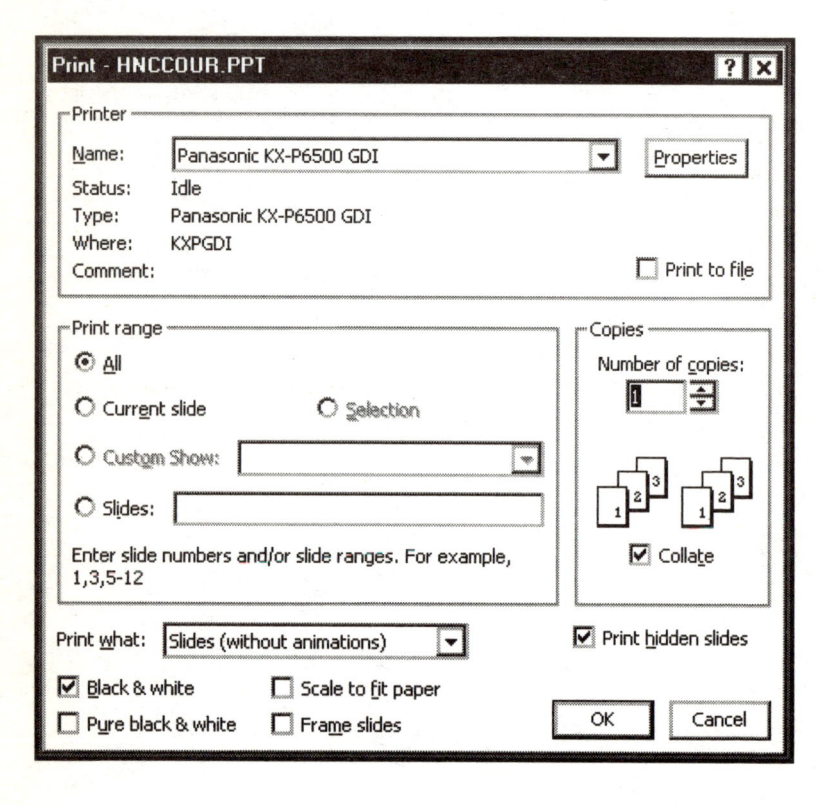

Print What
You can output the file as :

- ☐ Individual slides (one to a page).
- ☐ Notes pages (the slides and the notes are printed for each slide).
- ☐ Handouts (2, 3 or 6 slides per page).
- ☐ Outline pages.

Print Hidden Files
You can hide certain slides within your presentation and only show them if you wish, selecting this option would include them in the printout.

Black & white
This makes all colour fills into B&W and borders all unbordered objects.

Scale to fit Paper
Alters the scale to fit the paper size being used.

Pure black & white
Makes everything B&W or grey scale.

Frame slides
This prints a frame around each slide.

Saving Your Work

You should get into the habit of saving your work regularly so that any problems, whether hardware or software, do not cause too much loss of time or other problems.

To save your work you can click on the **Save** button that is on the toolbar along the top of the screen.

The first time you save your file, you will see a dialog box asking for a file name.

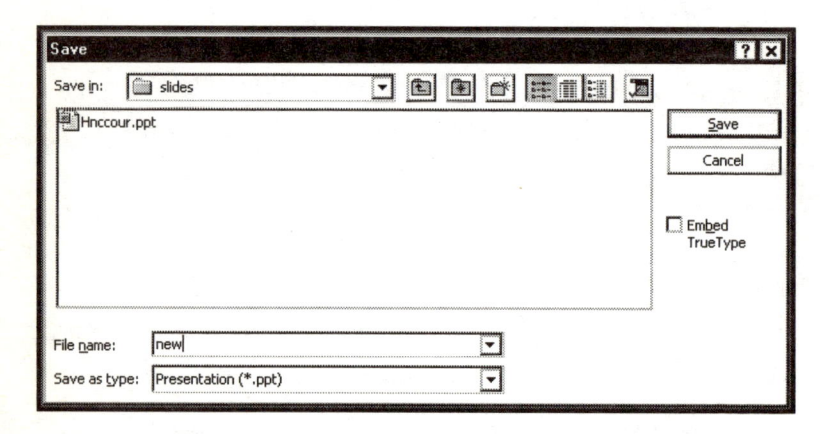

At this point, you can change where you save the file by clicking on the arrow to the right of **Save in** and alter the folder or disc you are saving to.

Next time you use the **Save** button to save your work the process will be automatic and there will be no dialog box appearing.

If you want to change the disc or folder or change the name of the file then click on the **File** command along the top of the screen and then on **Save As**. Also note the **Save as type** option, you can save your file in a variety of different formats so that it can be opened in another program.

Text

In this chapter, you will be looking at the various ways of entering and manipulating text within your presentation.

Entering Text

This is simple, just highlight the original text and type the text you want.

If you are starting with a blank presentation, then click where prompted and begin typing.

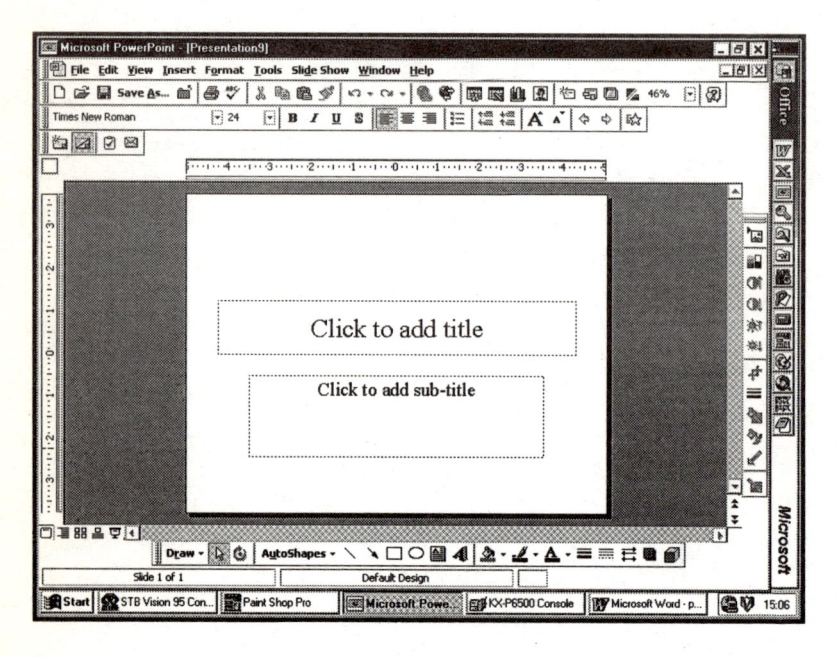

When entering body text use the **return** key to move on to the next point, a new bullet will appear below the original.

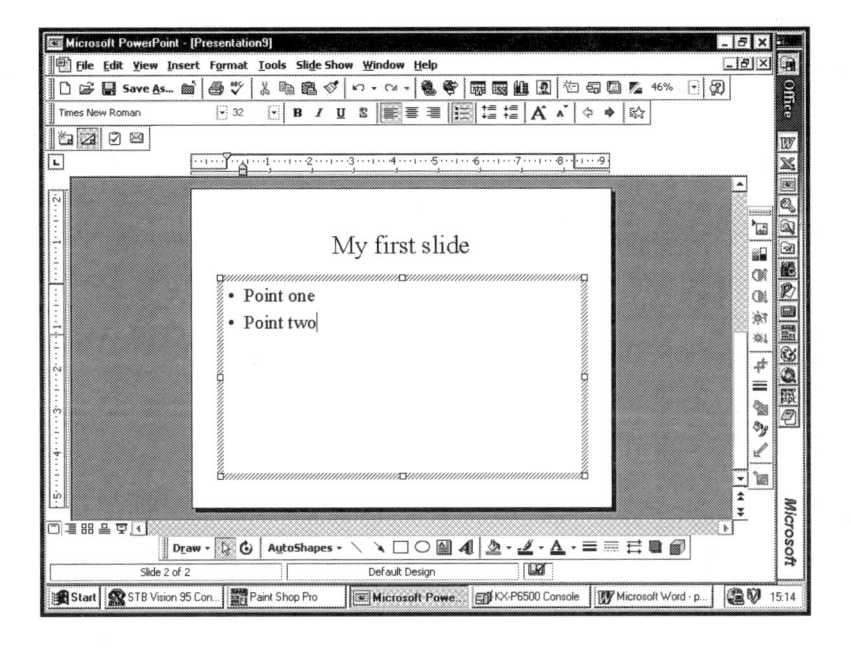

Altering the Font

Each design has fonts allocated to it, often these are ideal, but if you want to alter the fonts, there are three methods.

☐ Highlight the text (by clicking and dragging the mouse to highlight and select the text), then click on the **Font** button along the upper toolbar and choose another font. You can also alter the **Font Size**.

> Bookman Old Style ▾ 32 ▾

☐ Alter the **Master Slide** so that all the text within all the slides in the current file changes to the new font/font size (see section on master slides).

☐ Select the text and pull down the **Format** menu and select **Font**. This gives several choices.

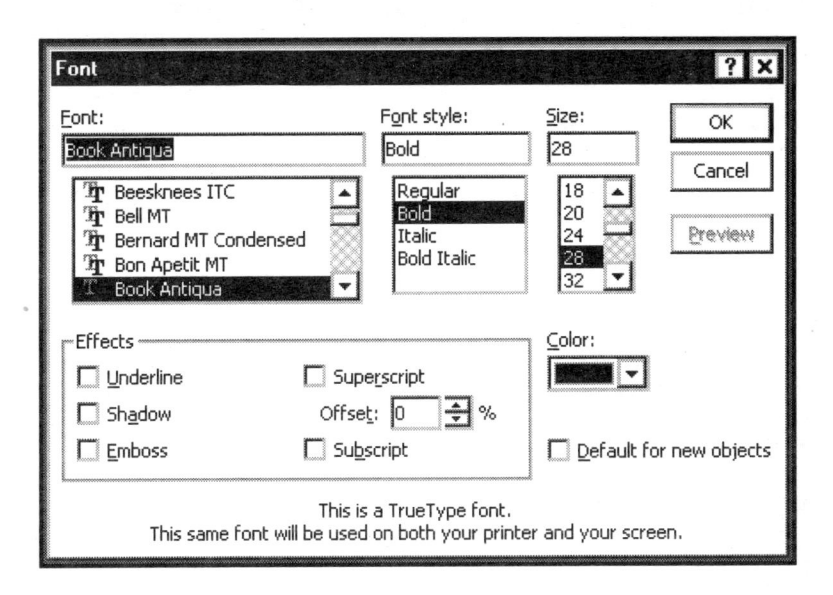

Font

Font: Book Antiqua

- Beesknees ITC
- Bell MT
- Bernard MT Condensed
- Bon Apetit MT
- Book Antiqua

Font style: Bold

- Regular
- Bold
- Italic
- Bold Italic

Size: 28

- 18
- 20
- 24
- 28
- 32

OK
Cancel
Preview

Effects
- ☐ Underline
- ☐ Shadow
- ☐ Emboss
- ☐ Superscript
- Offset: 0 %
- ☐ Subscript

Color:

☐ Default for new objects

This is a TrueType font.
This same font will be used on both your printer and your screen.

Spell Checking Your Text

It is very easy to destroy your presentation by using incorrect spelling. PowerPoint includes a spell checker that is accessed by clicking on the button along the upper toolbar.

A dialog box will appear.

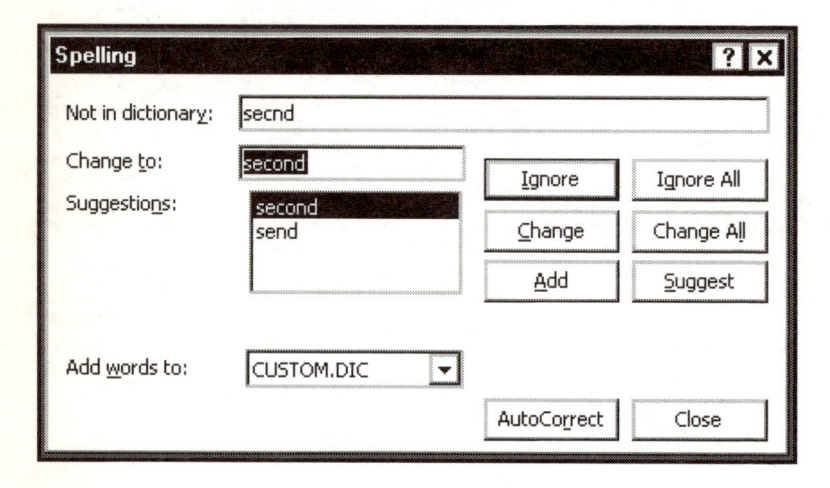

Spelling			? X
Not in dictionary:	secnd		
Change to:	second	Ignore	Ignore All
Suggestions:	second / send	Change	Change All
		Add	Suggest
Add words to:	CUSTOM.DIC		
		AutoCorrect	Close

The way a spell checker operates is to compare every word you enter against a (finite) list of words. If the word you type is not in the list, the spell checker program will identify it. This does not mean it is wrong, merely that it is not in the dictionary. You can **Add** words to your dictionary if you wish.

Adding Graphics & Objects

It is useful and rewarding to add visuals to your presentation. You can add:

☐ Clipart (from the library that comes with the program)

☐ Pictures or scanned images

☐ Graphs

☐ WordArt or objects such as an equation or a drawing you have made within Paintbrush or a chart from Excel

☐ Organisation Charts

☐ Other objects

Clipart

Select the slide you want to add the image to.

Click on the **Insert Clip Art** button on the toolbar.

You will see the **Microsoft Clip Gallery**.

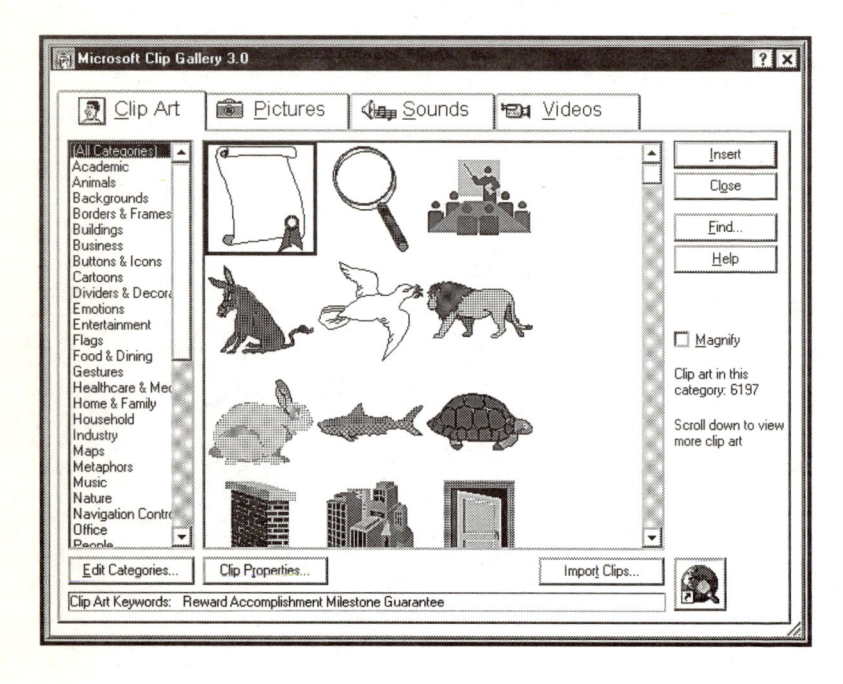

Select the image you want from the library and you will see it appear within the slide, it can then be altered.

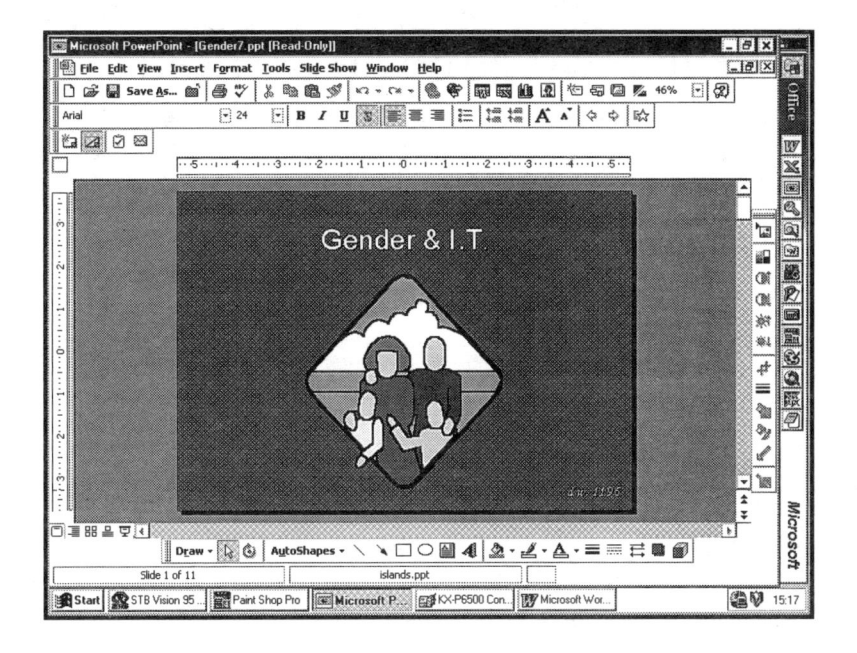

Adding pictures, sounds and videos

In a similar way to clip art, you can add (photograph quality) pictures, sounds and even video clips to your slide show.

These can be inserted using those installed in the **Clip Gallery** or you can insert them using the **Insert** menu.

A Word for Windows Table

This lets you easily create and import a table from Word. Click on the button on the toolbar.

A dialog box will appear that allows you to choose the number of rows and columns in the table.

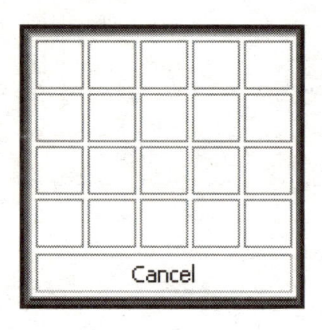

The table will then appear and you can enter whatever you want to within it (text, images, etc.) and format it as you wish.

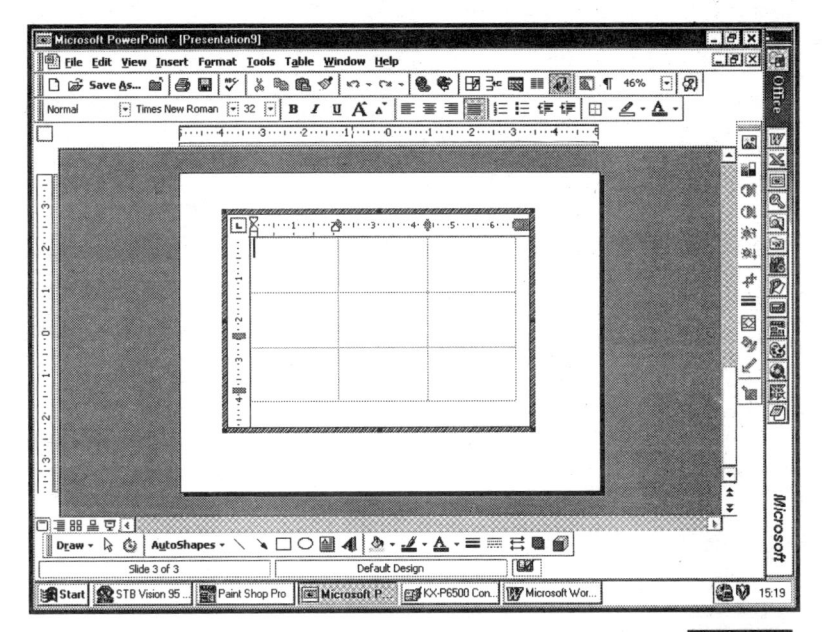

You can insert an Excel worksheet in a similar way.

Graphs

You can insert graphs by selecting **Insert, Object** and then **Microsoft Graph 97 Chart** or by clicking on the toolbar button.

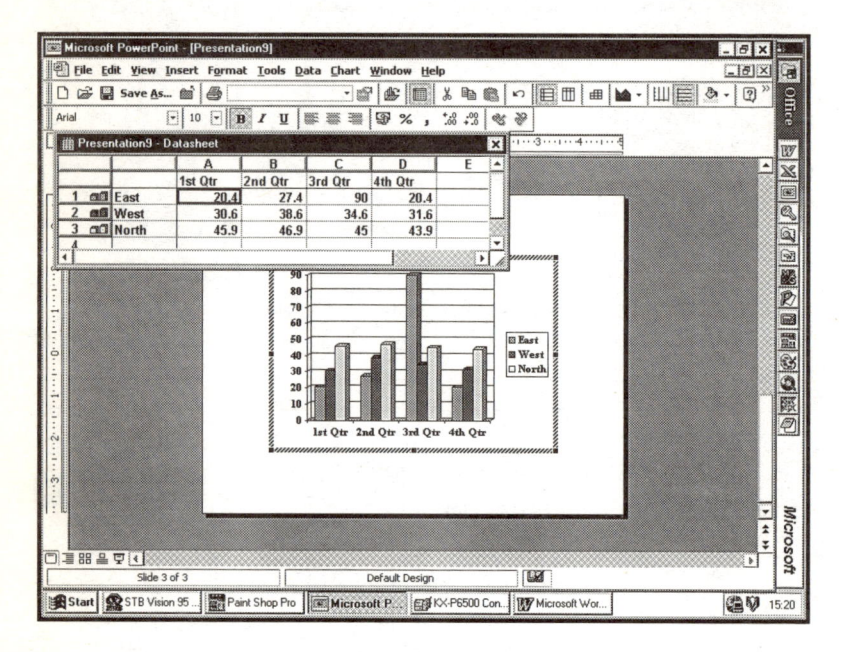

You will see the screen (above), this is **Microsoft Graph** (a mini application that can be accessed from all the main applications such as PowerPoint and Word).

You can create your own graph by altering and/or adding to the data shown.

Once you start the process you will see some new buttons appear on the toolbar.

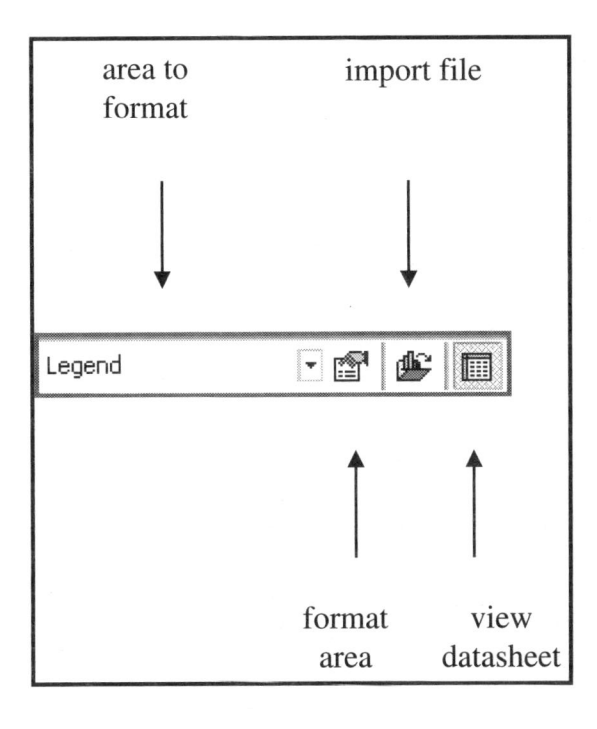

```
              area to            import file
              format
                 |                   |
                 ↓                   ↓
    ┌─────────────────────────────────────────┐
    │ Legend              ▼  📋  👆  📅        │
    └─────────────────────────────────────────┘
                         ↑        ↑
                         |        |
                       format    view
                        area    datasheet
```

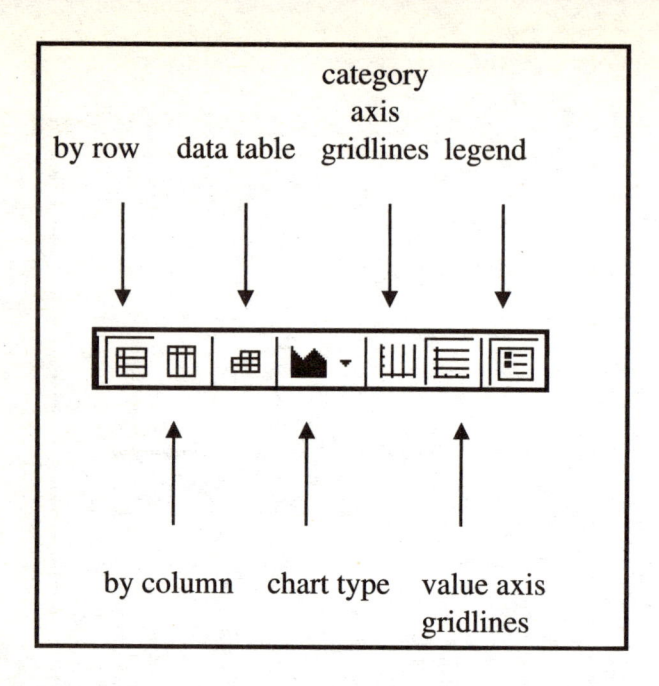

```
       by row    data table  category    legend
                             axis
                             gridlines
         ↓           ↓          ↓           ↓

       [toolbar icons]

              ↑          ↑          ↑
          by column  chart type  value axis
                                 gridlines
```

After entering the figures and text into the spreadsheet table, you can choose to improve your graph by using the various buttons and you can add text, etc. Graphs can be sized and so on in a similar way to other visuals.

Here is one I made earlier.

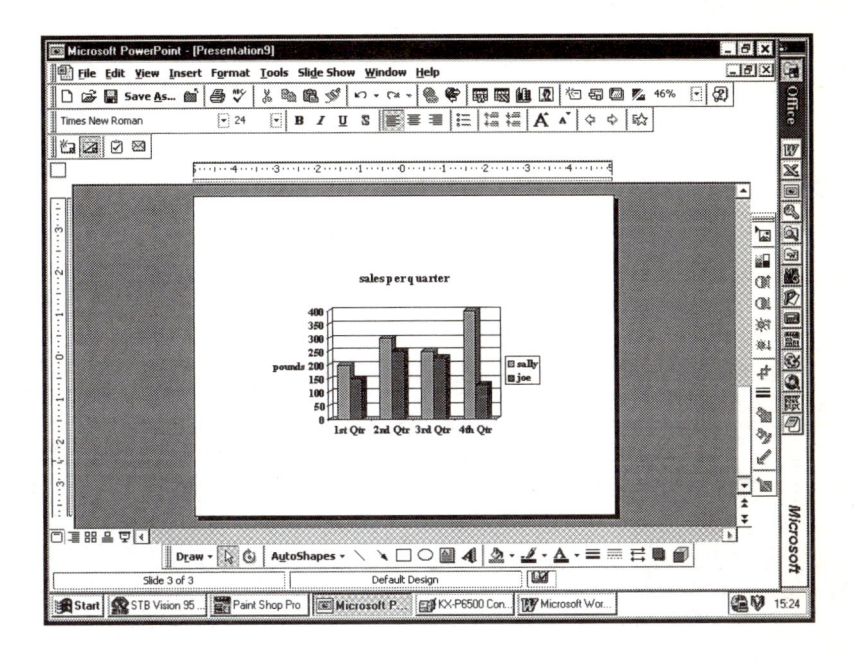

WordArt

Another type of object you can insert into your presentation is WordArt. You can create special text effects and fancy lettering for logos or titles by using this.

To start off, pull down the **Insert** menu and then **Object** and then **Microsoft WordArt 3**. After creating a frame with the **WordArt** tool, the **WordArt** program will be loaded automatically.

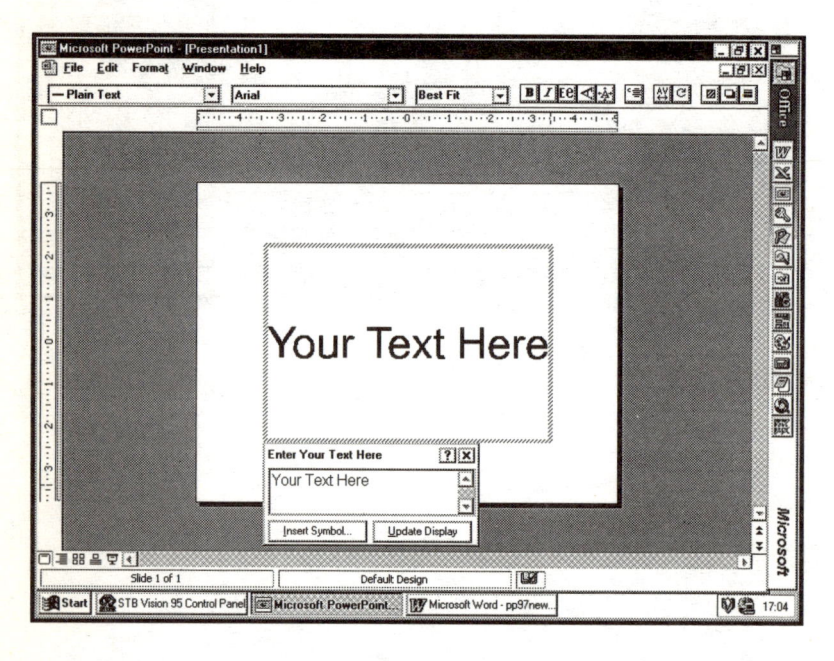

The screen shows the addition of a text entry box and additional buttons that appear on the upper toolbar.

You enter your text in the box (returning to create a new line) and then use the buttons to create the effect you want.

An explanation of the buttons follows (it is a good idea to experiment with the effect you can create using these buttons).

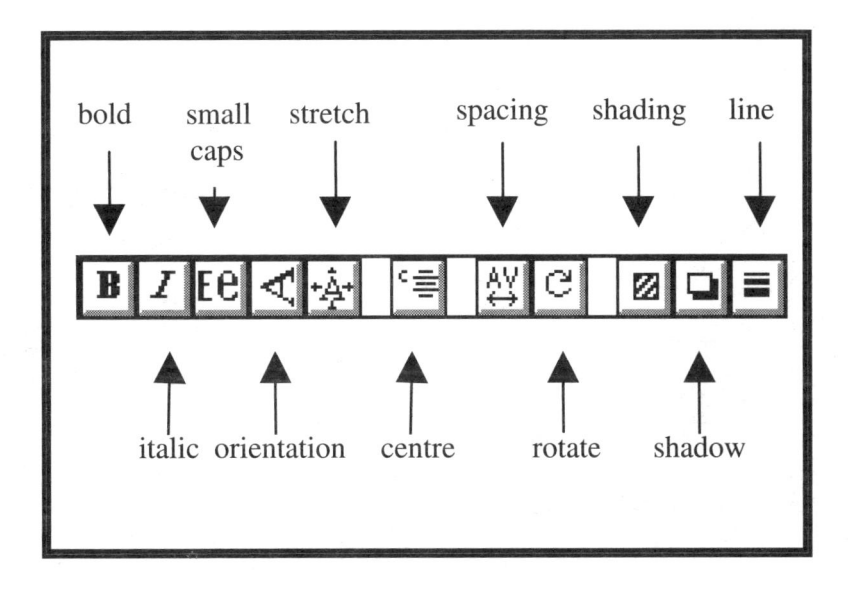

```
bold   small   stretch      spacing   shading   line
       caps
 ↓      ↓       ↓             ↓         ↓        ↓
[B][I][Ee][◁][⁺A⁺][‗≡][AV][C][▨][▢][≡]
     ↑      ↑          ↑         ↑         ↑
   italic orientation centre   rotate   shadow
```

Once you have finished the text and effects, just click the mouse away from the object and WordArt will close down and you will return to the original screen.

To alter your WordArt object double-click it and WordArt will be loaded again.

Here is an example of the use of WordArt.

There is another method of inserting (a slightly different version of) WordArt into a presentation and this is dealt with in the **Drawing toolbar** section.

Organisation Charts

One of the advantages of a program such as PowerPoint is the variety of predesigned diagrams and other graphics available.

To insert an organisation chart into your presentation, pull down the **Insert** menu and select **Object**, followed by **MS Organisation Chart 2**.

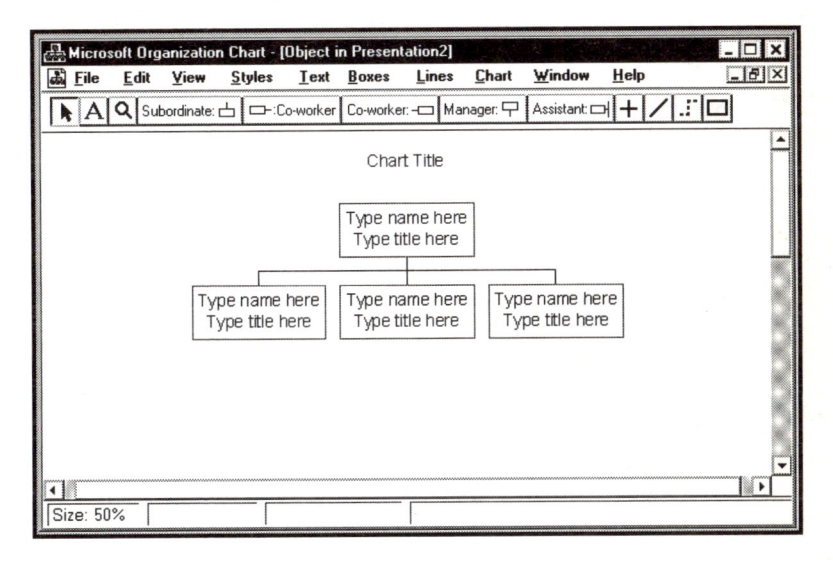

You enter the names and titles by highlighting the relevant text and overtyping.

File Menu

```
New                                 Ctrl+N
Open...                             Ctrl+O
Close and Return to Presentation2

Update Presentation2
Save Copy As...
Revert...

Exit and Return to Presentation2
```

The new commands are :

Update Presentation
This updates the organisation chart in PowerPoint to be the same as the one you are working with in the Organisation Chart screen.

Revert
This discards any changes you have made since the last time you saved the chart.

Edit
The new commands are **Select** and **Select Levels**. These enable you to select boxes within the chart.

You can also select all or part of the chart by clicking and dragging the mouse over the boxes you want to select.

View

You can size the chart and also display the **Draw** tools (specific to the chart) which can be very useful to add lines, etc., to an organisation chart.

Styles

The menu show you a series of group styles which you can apply to any box(es) within your chart (that you have selected).

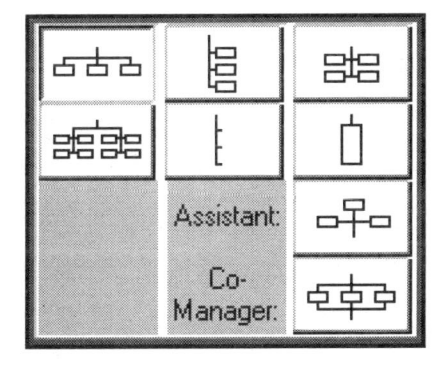

Text

Within this menu, you can alter the alignment, font or colour of **selected** text.

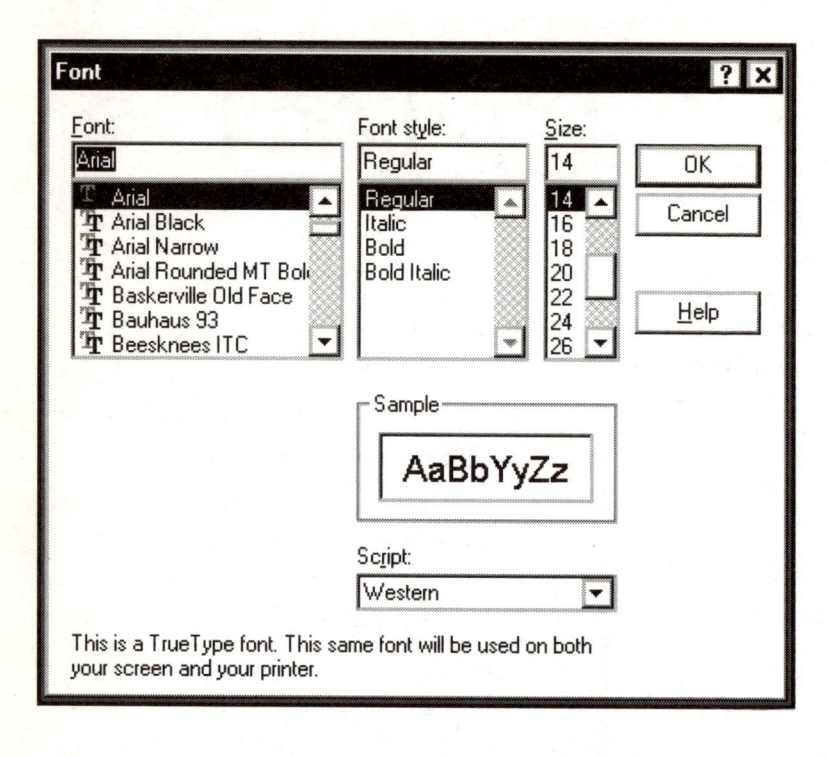

Boxes

Similarly, you can alter the look of selected boxes by altering the lines, borders, colours, etc.

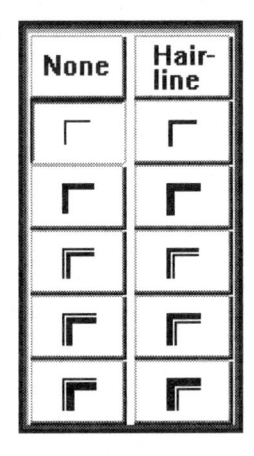

Lines

Here you can alter the line styles (thickness, colour, etc.) for selected lines.

Chart

This lets you change the background colour.

Help

The organisation chart screen has its own specific help.

Toolbar Buttons
The new buttons found within the Organisation Chart screen are explained here.

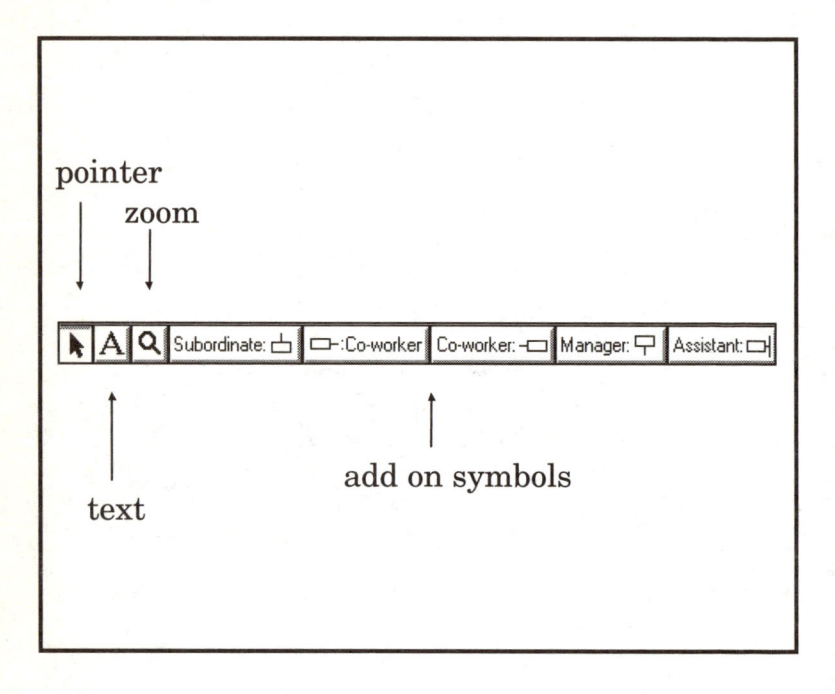

pointer

zoom

text

add on symbols

Add On Symbols
These can be added to any **selected** box to customise the chart to portray the organisational structure you want.

Other Objects

There are several other objects you can add to your presentation, for example **Microsoft Note-It** (the computer equivalent of sticky labels) and the **Microsoft Equation 3** (using this you can enter very complex mathematical symbols and equations).

Artwork

Manipulating Images
There are various techniques that can be used to enhance the image (and these techniques can be applied to most visuals and objects).

Moving an Image or Other Object
Make sure that the image has been selected (it should have little squares around it) then click the mouse within the image and *while holding down the mouse button* move to a new position.

Sizing an Image or Object
There are two ways to achieve this.

- ☐ Select the image and then position the mouse pointer on one of the small squares surrounding the image. The mouse pointer should become a small line with arrows at either end. While keeping the mouse button held down, move the mouse either in or out to resize the image.

☐ Select the image, pull down the **Format** menu, and select **Picture** or **Object**. You will see a dialog box, all you need to do is to enter the percentage you want to scale to.

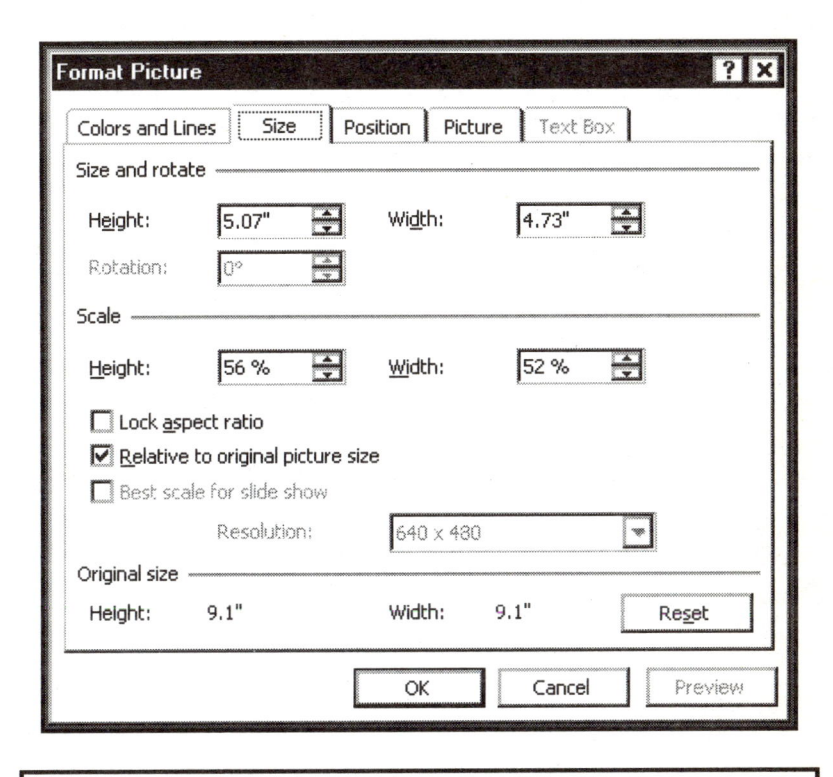

```
Format Picture                                           [?][X]
┌─────────────────────────────────────────────────────────────┐
│ Colors and Lines │ Size │ Position │ Picture │ Text Box │
│ ─ Size and rotate ────────────────────────────────────── │
│   Height:  [5.07"]     Width:  [4.73"]                      │
│   Rotation: [0°]                                            │
│ ─ Scale ─────────────────────────────────────────────────── │
│   Height:  [56 %]      Width:  [52 %]                       │
│   ☐ Lock aspect ratio                                       │
│   ☑ Relative to original picture size                       │
│   ☐ Best scale for slide show                               │
│        Resolution:  [640 x 480]                             │
│ ─ Original size ────────────────────────────────────────── │
│   Height:   9.1"       Width:   9.1"        [ Reset ]       │
│                                                             │
│              [  OK  ]  [ Cancel ]  [ Preview ]              │
└─────────────────────────────────────────────────────────────┘
```

You can size **Relative to original** (which is the default setting and keeps the correct proportions) or scale for the **Best scale for slide show** to optimise the image for viewing within the slide show.

Cropping an Object

Cropping is different from sizing. Sizing makes the whole image smaller (or bigger), but when you crop an object, you remove part of the whole object.

This is sometimes useful to remove extraneous parts of a picture or other image.

To do this view the **Picture** toolbar and the cropping tool will be shown.

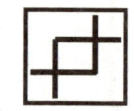

You then grab any corner of your object with the tool and remove part of the object..

> You can bring back any part of a cropped image in the same way you removed it.

Here are two images, one before cropping and one after.

To achieve this I copied the original image then cropped each to leave the faces, some of the second image had to be recoloured to remove part of the image by making it white.

> You can also crop by selecting the image and then pulling down the **Format** menu, selecting **Picture or Object** and then **Picture**.

Altering Your Slides

Some of the ways of altering your slides have already been covered, for example changing the design; this chapter deals with the various other methods of customising the look of your presentation so that it stands out from other presentations.

Making Changes to the Master Slide

You can alter individual slides or you can make changes to all the slides by amending the **Master** slide.

To do this, pull down the **View** menu and select **Master**. You will be able to choose which type of master you alter from the list shown below.

> <u>S</u>lide Master
> <u>T</u>itle Master
> Han<u>d</u>out Master
> <u>N</u>otes Master

You will then see the **Master** appear and any changes or additions you make to this will be reflected in the master you have altered and all the slides making up the presentation.

Below is an example of a **Slide Master** with the date added and moved to the bottom left of the slide. See how the date is displayed, this means that it will be the date the file is printed or displayed, not the day it was created.

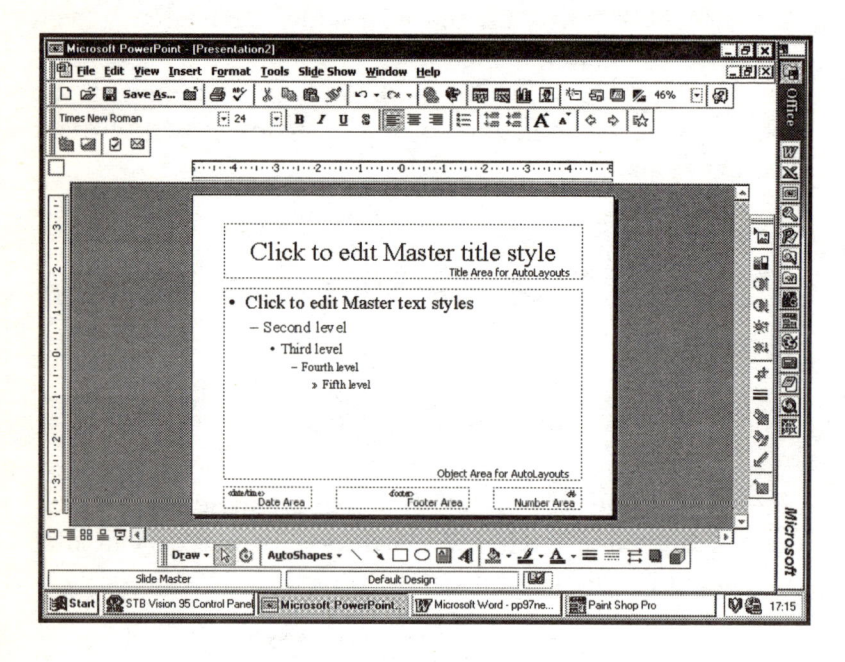

Deleting Slides

This can be achieved in two ways.

☐ In **Slide Sorter View** select the slide or slides by clicking on them and press the **Delete** key.

☐ In **Slide View** pull down the **Edit** menu and then select **Delete Slide**.

Drawing toolbar

If you are doing any work with graphics, then you will want to display the **Drawing** toolbar. I work with it permanently displayed.

> To display any toolbar, pull down the **View** menu and select **Toolbars**. Click on your choice. The toolbar will be displayed.

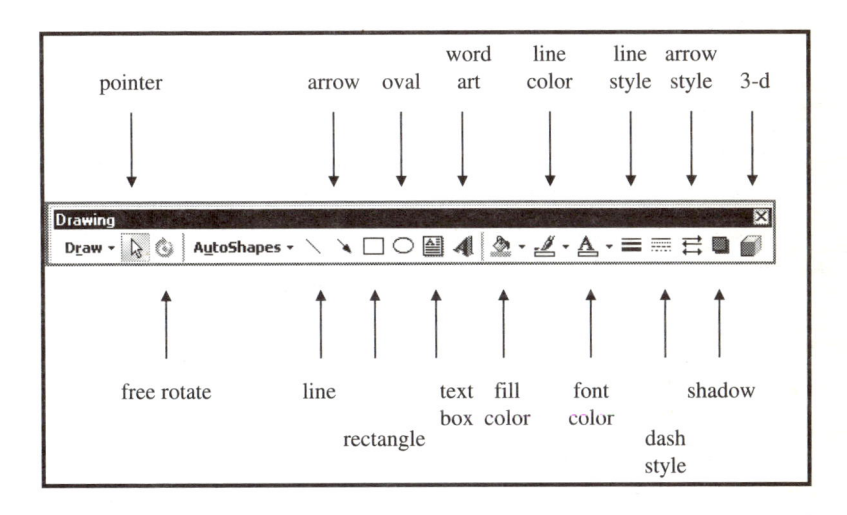

```
                        word   line   line  arrow
pointer      arrow oval art   color  style style  3-d
  ↓            ↓    ↓    ↓      ↓      ↓     ↓    ↓
[Drawing toolbar image]
  ↑            ↑         ↑  ↑          ↑          ↑
free rotate  line      text fill      font      shadow
                       box  color     color
                  rectangle                   dash
                                              style
```

There are some very useful tools here, for example you can add text boxes and arrows to any part of your slides.

Most of these are self-explanatory, however some are worth further investigation.

Draw

If you click on this, a further menu is displayed.

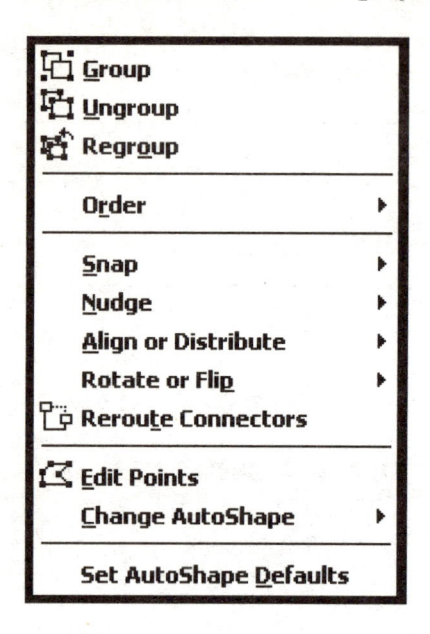

```
Group
Ungroup
Regroup

Order           ▶

Snap            ▶
Nudge           ▶
Align or Distribute  ▶
Rotate or Flip  ▶
Reroute Connectors

Edit Points
Change AutoShape ▶

Set AutoShape Defaults
```

Grouping and Ungrouping

You may want to use only a part of an image or you may want to rearrange the component parts of it.

To do this, select the image and then choose **Ungroup**.

A message *may* appear on the screen, which you can (if you want to ungroup the image) agree to.

> It is not possible to ungroup certain types of image.

You will see that the image is now made up of many sub-images all identified by the little squares surrounding them.

Click outside the image and then click on any component and you can move it, recolour it, size it or delete it as you wish.

> To select more than one component or object, hold down the **Shift** key while clicking the mouse on each item you want to select.

The illustration below shows the original image, look at page 69 to see how ungrouping and manipulating images can have a dramatic effect.

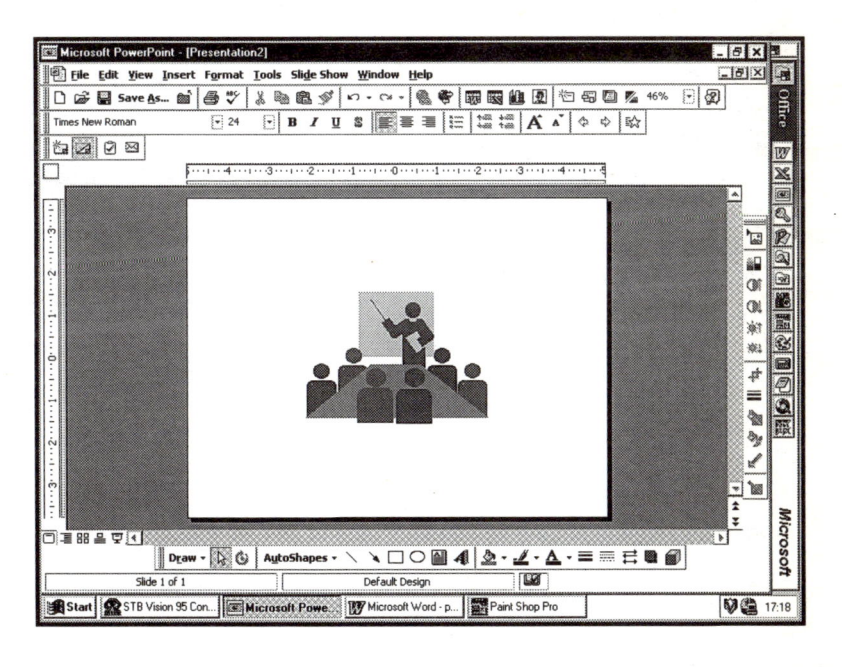

When you want to merge several images or objects into one so that they form a single group, which can be moved or resized as a single item, you can do this in several ways.

- Hold down the mouse button and drag the mouse around the items. This will select all the items.

- **or**

- While holding down the **shift** key, click the mouse on each item you want to include within the group.

- **or**

- Pull down the **Edit** menu and choose **Select All**.

Then (whichever method is used) choose **Group** or **Regroup** from the **Draw** menu.

Superimposing One Image on Another

A useful technique is to use two or more images to create a new one.

Insert the two images and carry out any sizing, ungrouping or sizing you wish to.

Select one of the images and move it physically over the other.

Below is an example of two images used together, the original one was ungrouped, one part deleted and the components moved around, the blackboard was recoloured. The second image, the donkey, was sized and then moved onto the blackboard.

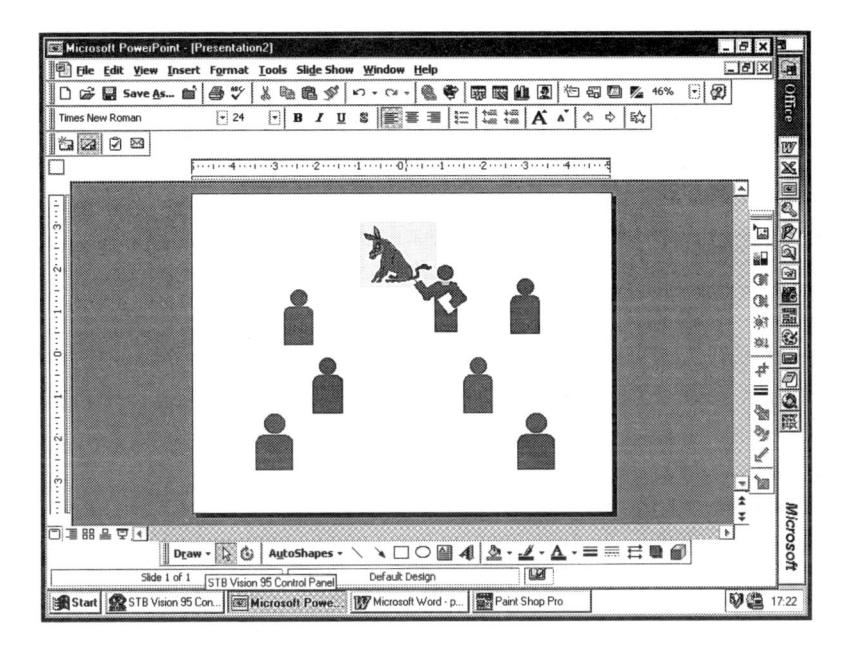

Order

You may want to place one object on top of another, the order in which these can be displayed can be critical to the result.

Think of the objects as being stacked, one on top of the next. The commands to vary the sequence are :

Bring to Front
This brings the selected object to the top of the pile.

Send to Back
This sends the selected object to the bottom of the pile.

Bring Forward
This brings the selected object forward one level in the pile.

Send Backward
This sends the selected object back one level in the pile.

Snap

There is an (invisible) grid and any object or text aligns itself to this. It makes lining up easier to achieve but does reduce fine control.

You can turn the **Snap to Grid** or **Snap to Shape** features on or off by selecting it (**Draw** and then **Snap**).

Nudge

If you have selected an object, you can nudge it in various directions.

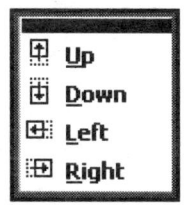

```
⊞ Up
⊞ Down
⊞ Left
⊞ Right
```

Align or Distribute

This is used to align objects and/or text, you have to have selected more than one object or text for this to be usable, then simply pull down the **Draw** menu and **Align**. You have a choice of alignments and you can experiment with this technique.

To select more than one item hold down the Shift key while clicking the items.

Save the file before making any experimental changes to it.

Rotate or Flip

You can rotate or flip objects within PowerPoint. To do so, select the **Draw** menu and select **Rotate or Flip**. You will be given the following choices.

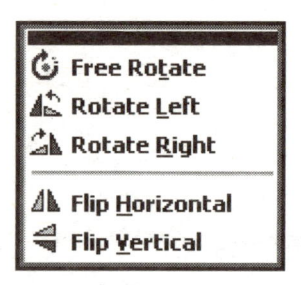

- Free Rotate
- Rotate Left
- Rotate Right
- Flip Horizontal
- Flip Vertical

Free Rotate lets you grab any of the corners with the rotate tool and rotate to your heart's desire. Below is an example (the donkey has been flipped).

> If your image will not allow you to choose **Rotate or Flip** then if you **Ungroup** it (**Draw** menu) and then **Group** it again, it becomes a PowerPoint object and can be rotated.

Rotating Text

As well as being able to rotate objects, PowerPoint enables you to rotate text.

To do this simply select the text and use the **Drawing** toolbar, select **Draw** and then **Rotate or Flip**.

Edit Points

If you have created a freeform shape (e.g. by using any of the freeform tools (shown opposite) in the **AutoShapes Lines**), you can then move or edit the points within that object.

Change AutoShape

If you have created an AutoShape, and you select this option (while the AutoShape object is still selected) then you can choose another shape and the original shape will be converted into the new one.

AutoShapes and other shapes

The AutoShapes menu is shown below.

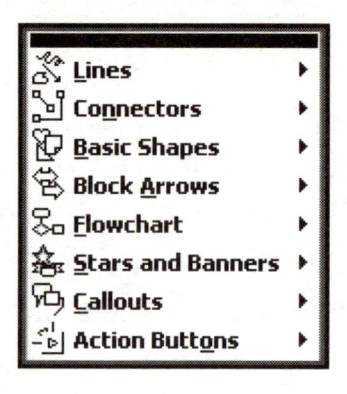

- Lines
- Connectors
- Basic Shapes
- Block Arrows
- Flowchart
- Stars and Banners
- Callouts
- Action Buttons

Each of these displays AutoShapes. The Flowchart shapes are shown for reference.

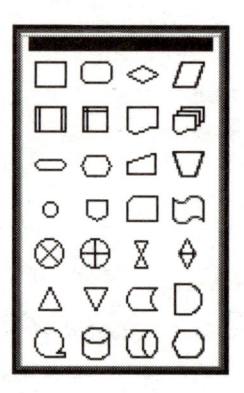

You select the symbol you want and then click and drag to produce the shape.

Once you have done this, you can manipulate the image as you wish, e.g. alter the shape, the colour and so on.

WordArt

If you click on the WordArt button on the **Drawing** toolbar, you will see a display of imaginative layouts.

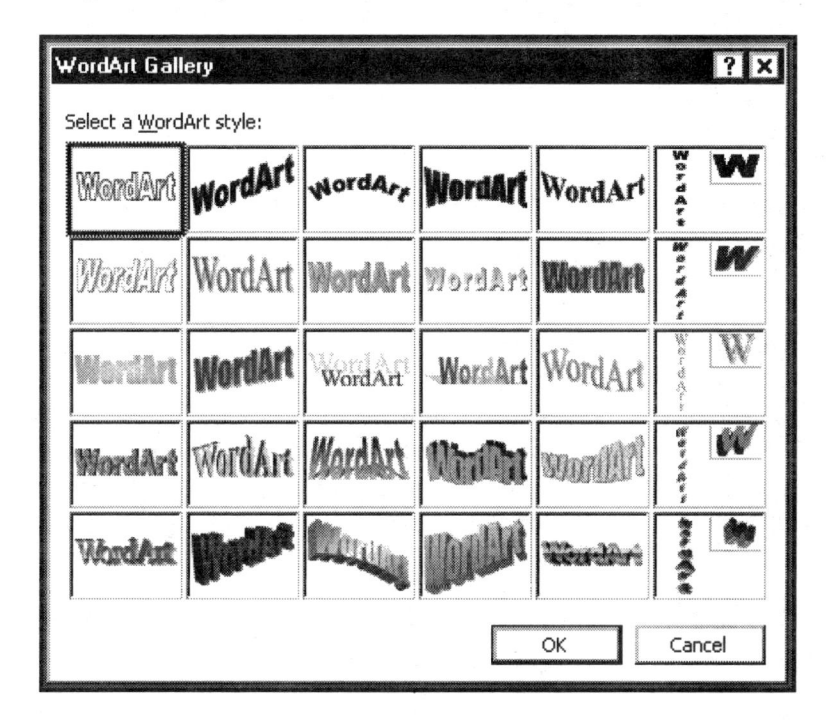

Choose the style, click on OK, enter your text in the dialog box that follows and you have your fancy text.

Creating Web Pages

Existing presentations

You can save an existing presentation as an HTML file and convert your existing presentation into a series of web pages.

The **Wizard** is described below (**Saving a PowerPoint file as HTML**).

Online designs

When you start the program, select **Template** from the dialog box, you should see the **Presentation Designs** screen. Then click on **Presentations** to view the various choices.

However, if you are already using PowerPoint and want to use the designs to create web pages, pull down the **File** menu and select **New** and then click on the **Presentations** tab and the various (both normal and on-line) presentation designs will be shown.

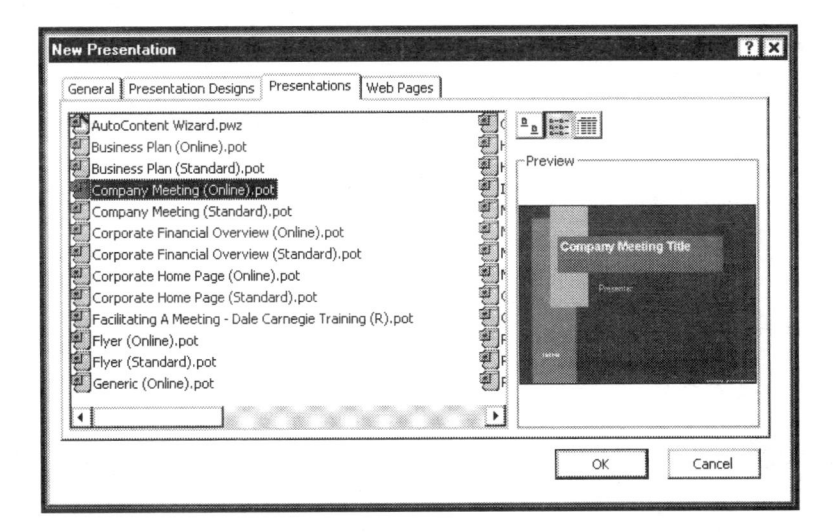

Note the three buttons on the right, these allow you to look at the list in different ways (as **Large Icons**, as a **List** and as a list in more **Detail**).

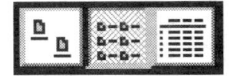

You choose (an **Online** design) from the list (remember that you can preview each by clicking on the title and you can see how it looks in the preview box to the right).

It is a good idea to look closely at the list, as there are a variety of different business and personal on-line designs. Remember that a design is only a starting point and you can alter the finished result.

You can then create your presentation normally and then save it as an HTML file by pulling down the **File** menu and selecting **Save as HTML**.

An example of an on-line design is shown below.

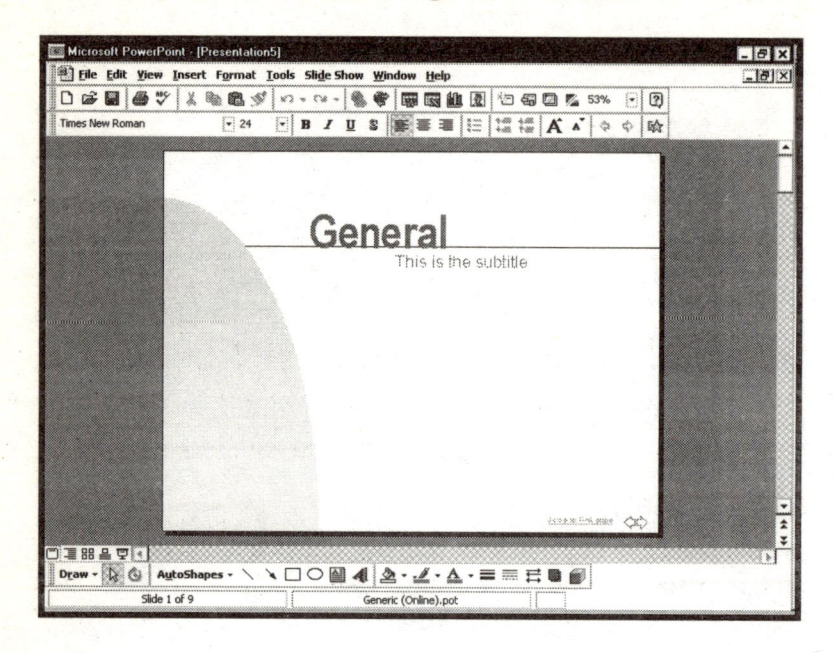

Saving a PowerPoint file as HTML

You can save your file using the **File** menu, followed by **Save as HTML**. There is a **Wizard** to assist you.

I have illustrated most of the **Wizard** screens and added explanations as they illustrate some fundamental points about creating web pages in PowerPoint.

The initial screen is shown below.

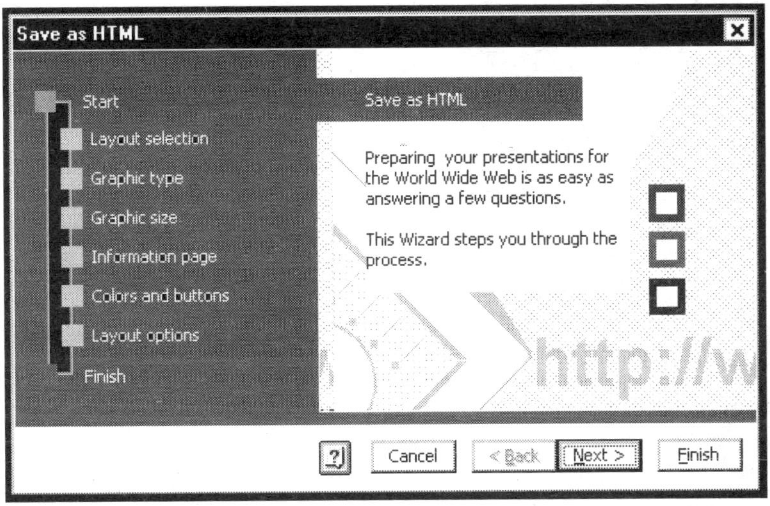

Save as HTML
Start
Layout selection
Graphic type
Graphic size
Information page
Colors and buttons
Layout options
Finish
Save as HTML
Preparing your presentations for the World Wide Web is as easy as answering a few questions.
This Wizard steps you through the process.
http://w
Cancel
< Back
Next >
Finish

This is followed by several screens asking you to make various choices. Some are illustrated and explained below.

The **page style** can be altered to **Browser frames**. This is a more sophisticated display and may not display properly in older versions of browsers.

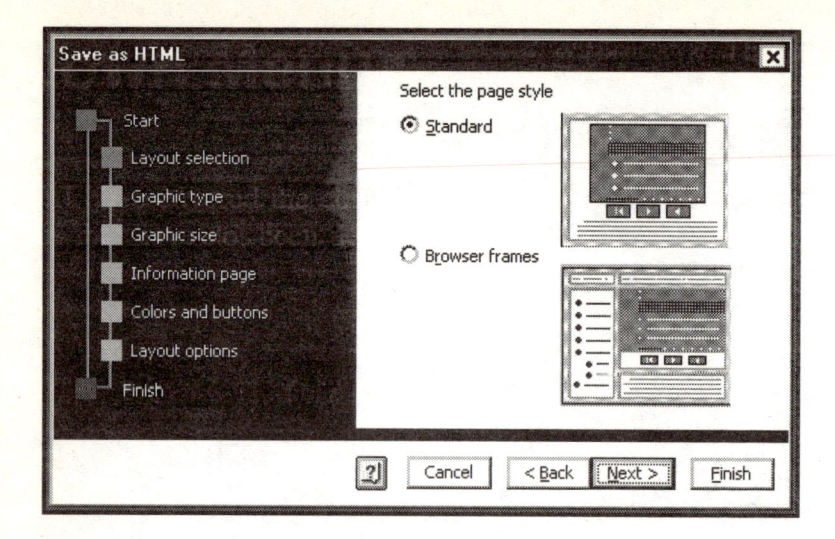

Frames are used where the designer wants to split the screen into various sections or frames that can operate independently.

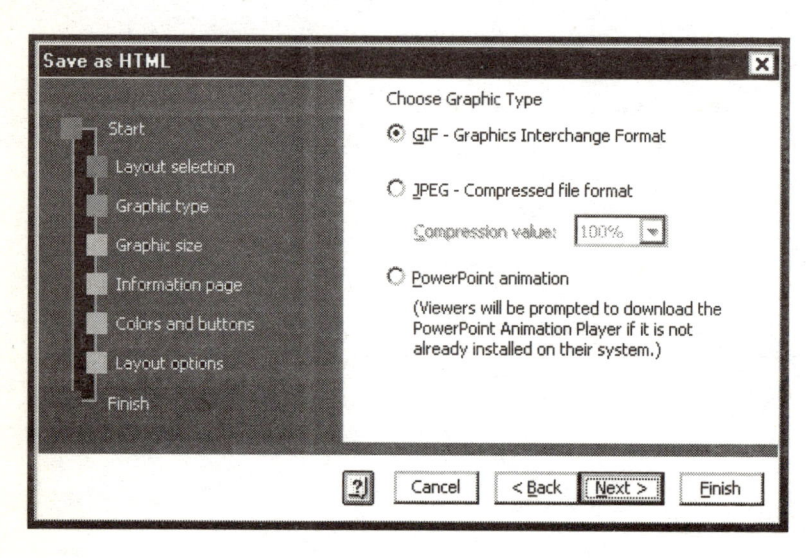

The graphics format you choose defines the quality of the image and its file size (GIF files tend to be better quality but may be larger in size, the quality and size of JPEG files depends upon the compression ratio - the higher the quality, the larger the size of file).

With graphics, there is always a trade off between file size, therefore the speed with which they can be viewed, and the quality of the image.

Note the previous screen, you can create web pages which retain and display the animations as part of the web page (the viewer may need to download a free Microsoft program to view the animations and they should automatically be prompted to do so).

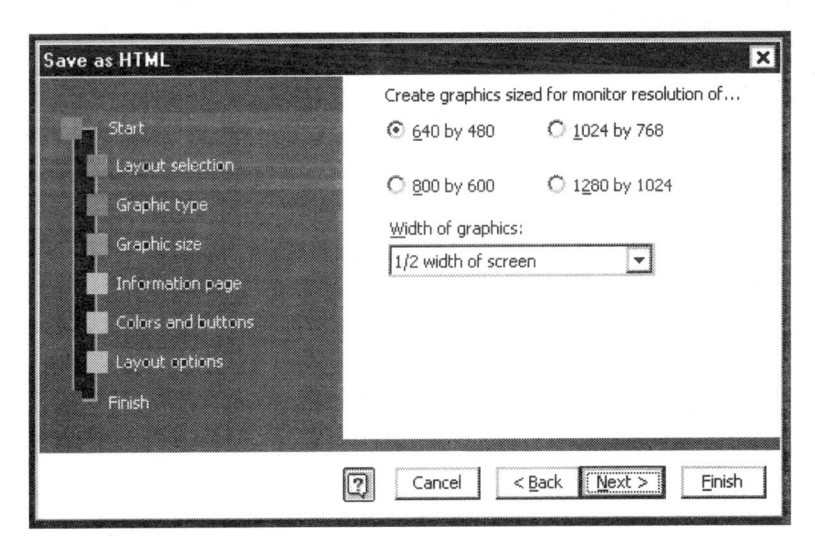

Be **very** careful here, if you alter the resolution be sure that the people viewing your web pages are operating at that (or a higher) resolution. Otherwise, they may only be able to see part of the image at any time.

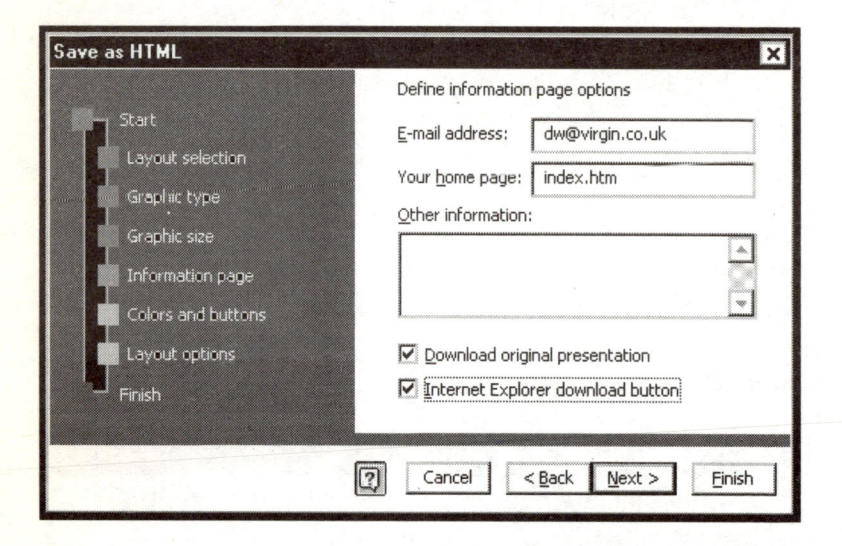

On this screen, enter your E-mail address and a home page file name (normally Index.htm). You can also add links to allow the user to download the presentation file and the latest version of Microsoft Explorer (if they want to).

The next page lets you alter the colours (the default is to use the browser colours as set by the viewer).

On the next screen, the design automatically adds buttons; here you can choose the style.

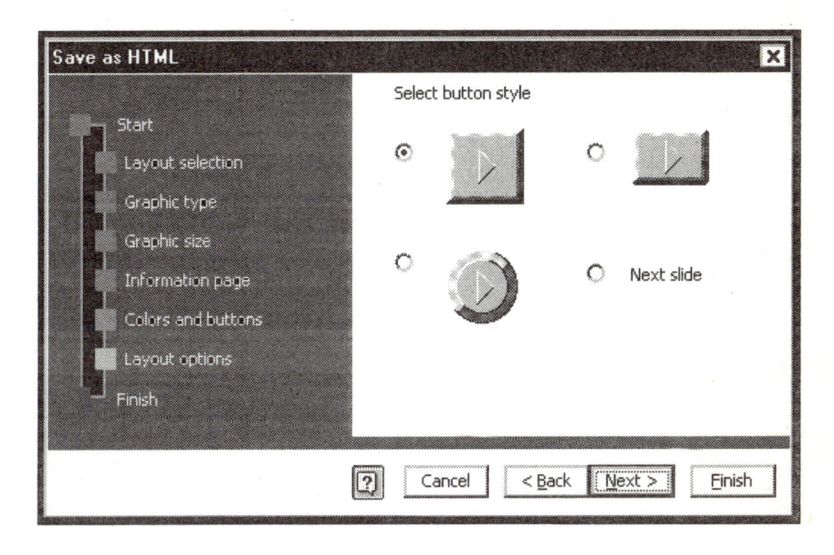

This screen lets you decide where to place the buttons that you chose in the previous screen.

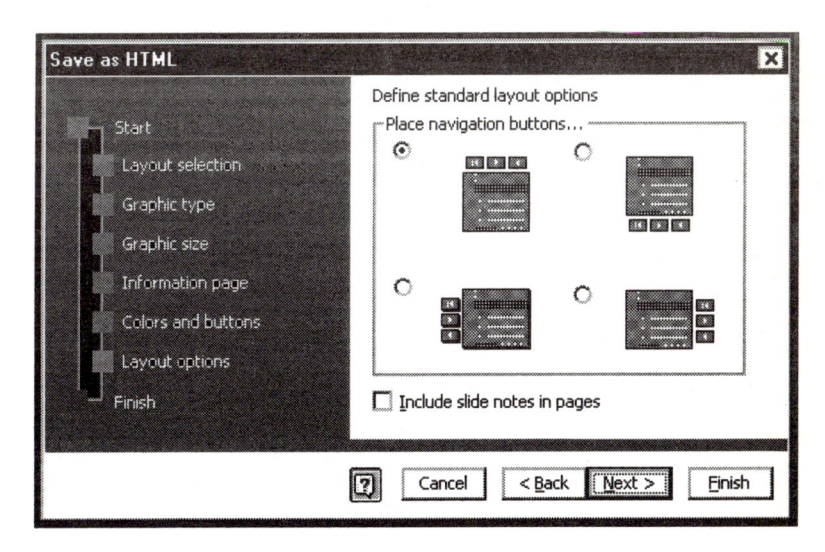

The final screen asks you to choose where to save the file.

If you want to see how it looks, you can open your browser and load the file.

The web presentation is saved in its own directory and comprises several files.

If you view the INDEX.HTM (this is created automatically), you will see an index to the slide show. An illustration is shown below.

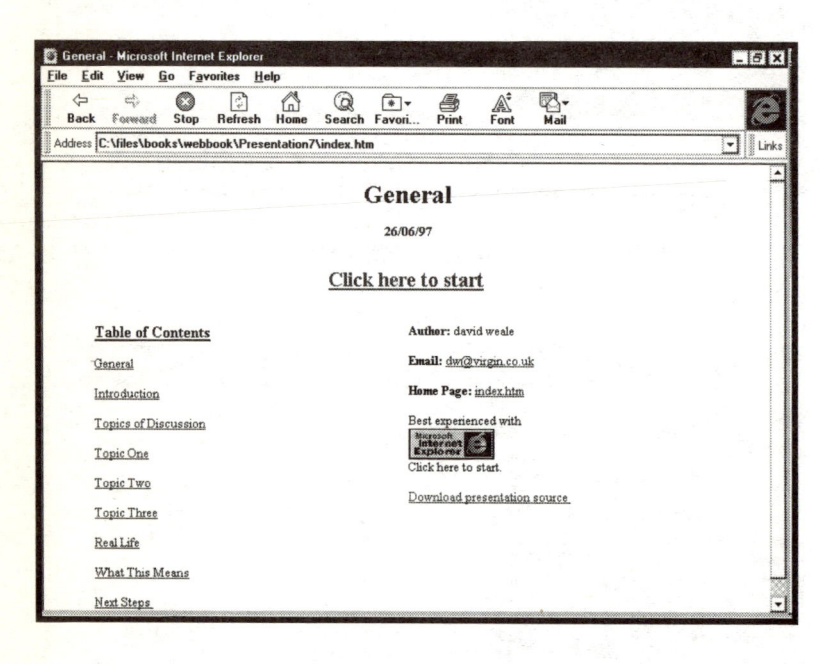

If you click on the **Click here to start** hyperlink then the slide show itself will begin.

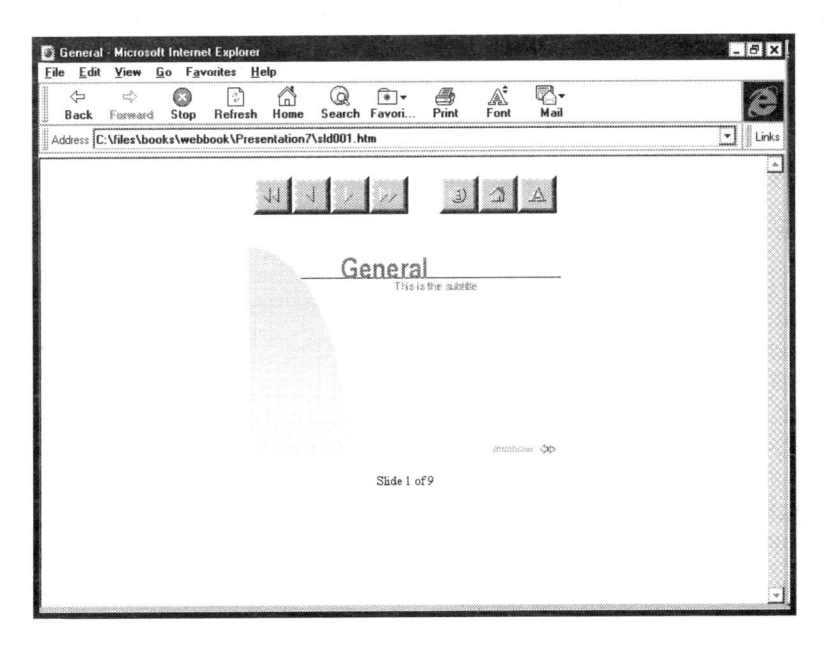

Banners

Another option within **File New** is **Web Pages**. If you select this, you will see that there are two banner files to choose from.

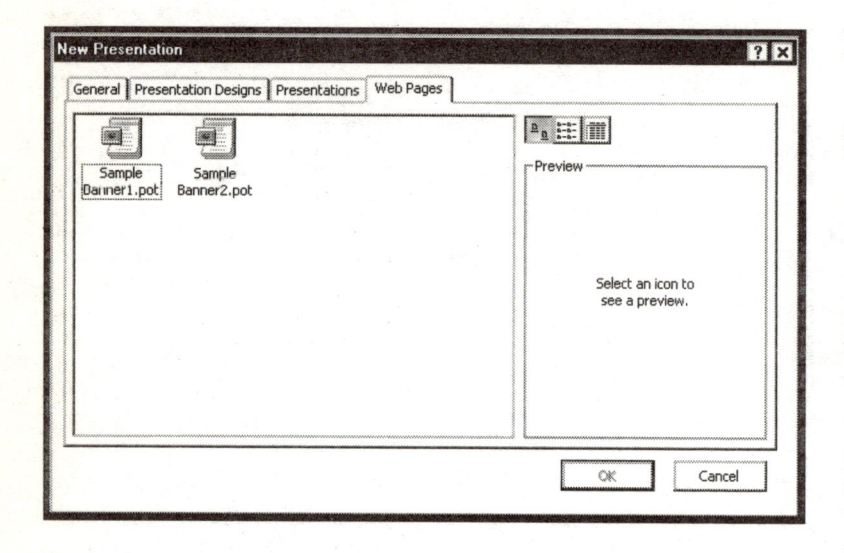

You can alter these banners as you wish and then save as HTML files to display on a browser. Each file consists of three slides, each with a different banner.

An example is shown below.

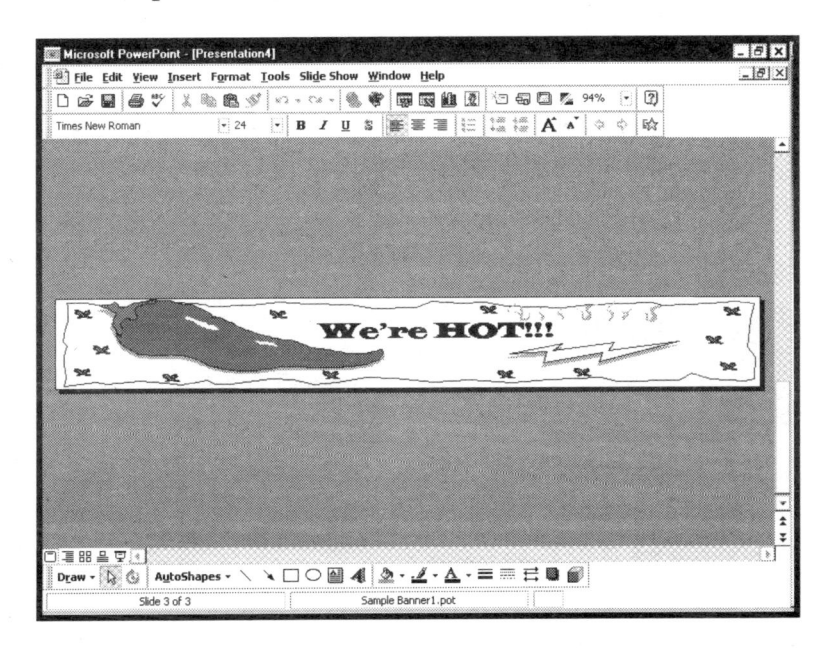

The Pull Down Menus

In this section of the book, I have covered the commands within the pull down menus that have not been dealt with previously.

File menu

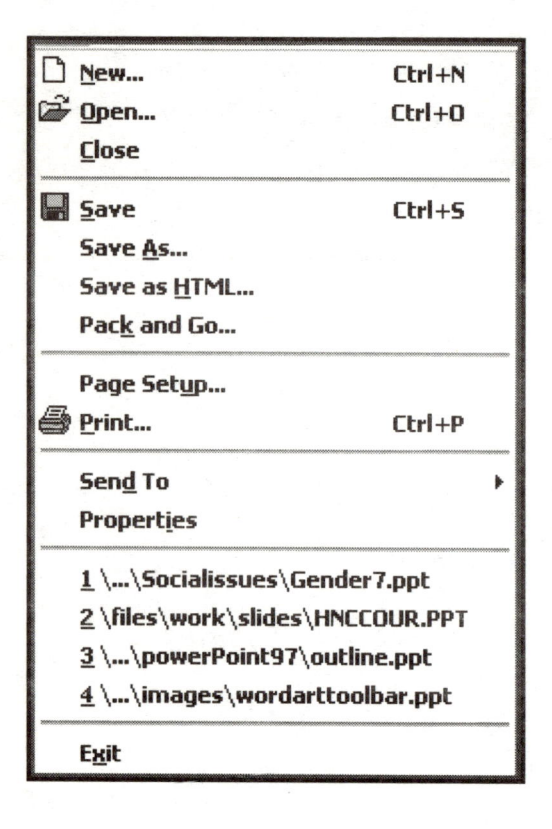

New...		Ctrl+N
Open...		Ctrl+O
Close		
Save		Ctrl+S
Save As...		
Save as HTML...		
Pack and Go...		
Page Setup...		
Print...		Ctrl+P
Send To		▶
Properties		
1 \...\Socialissues\Gender7.ppt		
2 \files\work\slides\HNCCOUR.PPT		
3 \...\powerPoint97\outline.ppt		
4 \...\images\wordarttoolbar.ppt		
Exit		

Pack and Go

This is very useful, especially if you are giving a presentation somewhere else and are unsure that they have PowerPoint. There is a **Wizard** to take you through the necessary steps. Certain of the screens are illustrated as they need some explanation.

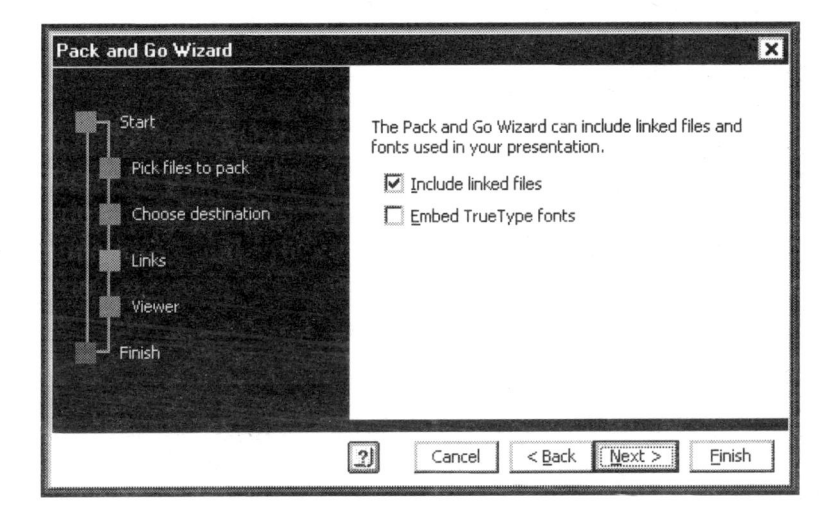

If you are unsure whether the host computer has the same fonts then you can choose to embed them within your file.

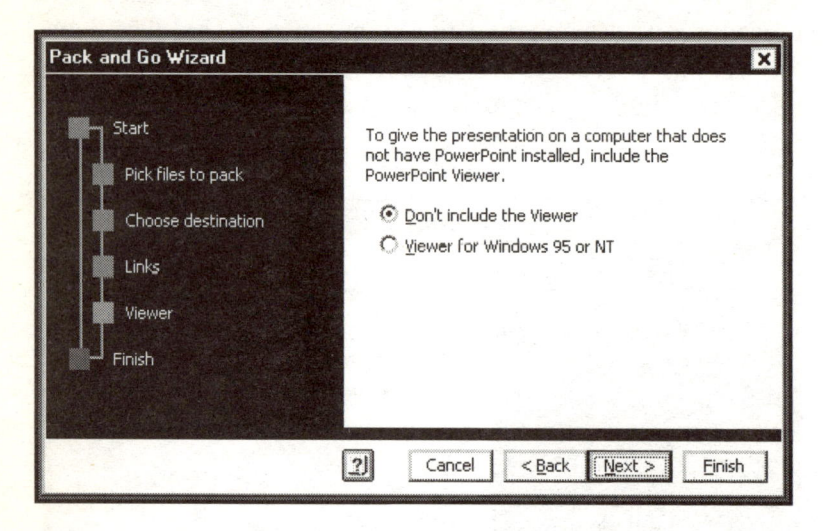

Again, if you are unsure whether the host computer has the same version of PowerPoint then you can include the **Viewer** (a small program that lets you view the slide show).

You need to be careful with the various versions and operating systems, you cannot, for example, use this technique with a Windows 3.1 machine as neither the file nor the viewer will be compatible (you need to save the file as a compatible version and use a compatible viewer).

> You may be prompted to use the **Office CD** to complete the process, depending the choices you made.

To unpack and run the slide show on another computer you need to follow these steps.

- Load **Windows Explorer** and look at the contents of drive A:.

- Double click the program **Pngsetup**

- Copy the presentation to the hard disc and then double click the PowerPoint Viewer to run the slide show.

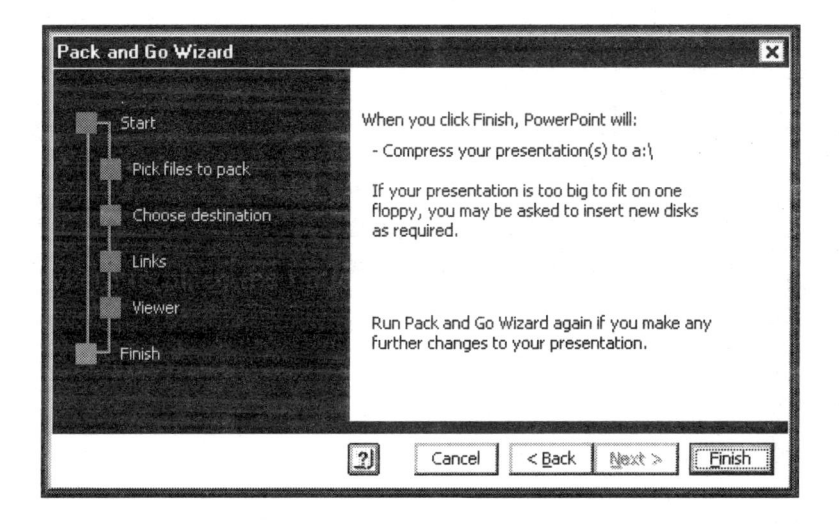

Send To

You can send a file to various places.

- Mail Recipient...
- Routing Recipient...
- Exchange Folder...
- Microsoft Word...

Mail Recipient

You can send the file via e-mail, if you select this option you will be asked to choose the **Profile**. This is the e-mail program you normally use.

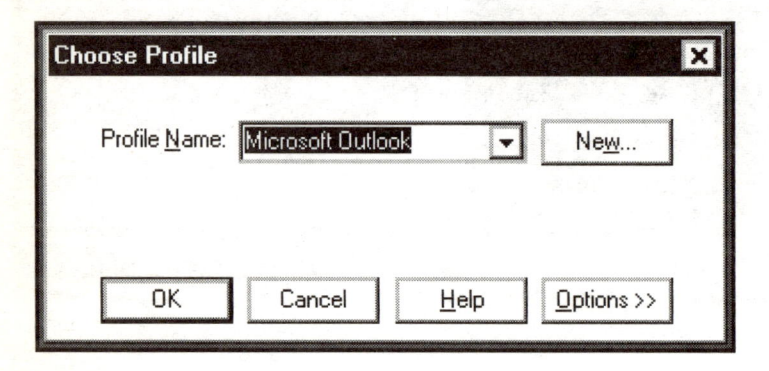

The e-mail program is then loaded and the file automatically included as an attachment.

With e-mail all the recipients receive a copy at the same time.

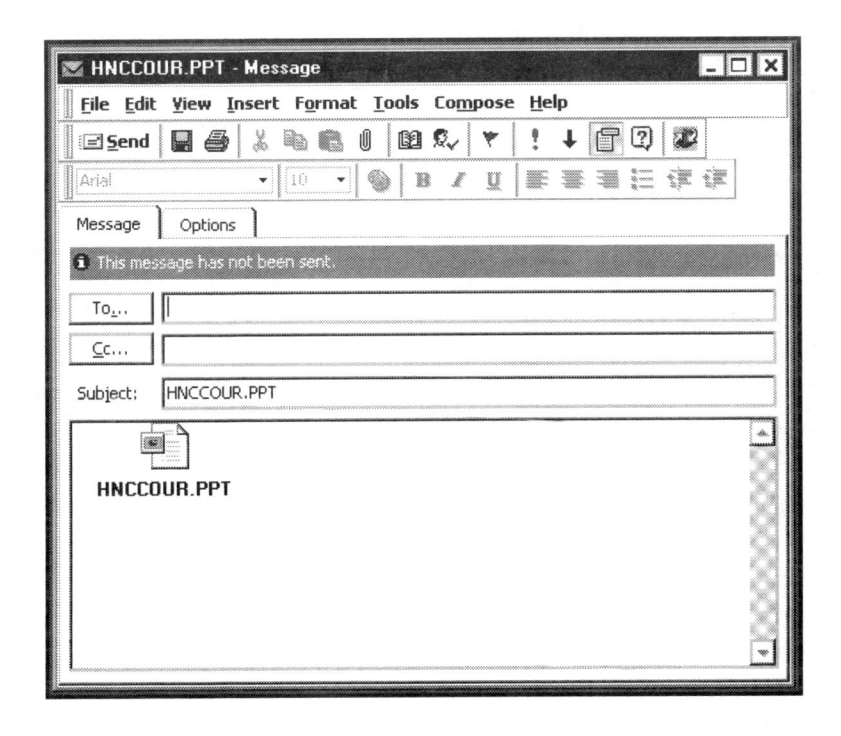

Routing Recipient

If you want the recipients to look at your file one at a time and (perhaps) add comments, then you can route the presentation to one recipient after another and each will see the previous comments. You can track the progress of the file and when it has been to all the recipients, it will automatically be returned to you.

If you select this option, a (**Routing Slip**) dialog box asking for the addresses of the recipients will be displayed.

Exchange Folder

You can post the file to a Microsoft Exchange public folder, so that anyone with access to the folder can look at the file.

You will be asked to select the folder, (you can create a new folder if you wish).

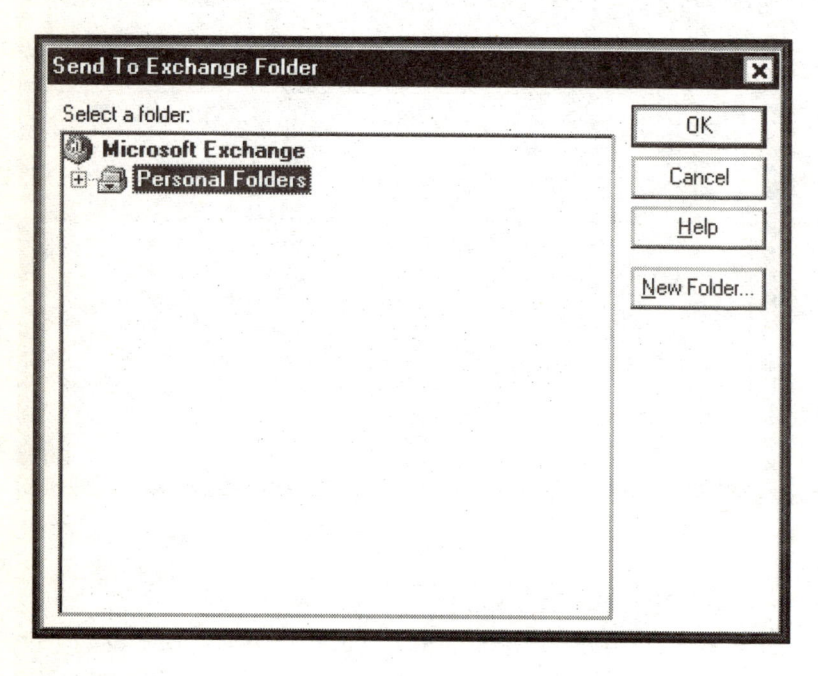

Microsoft Word

You can send the file to **Word**. You will see a dialog box, which gives you various choices about how the slides will appear within the Word document.

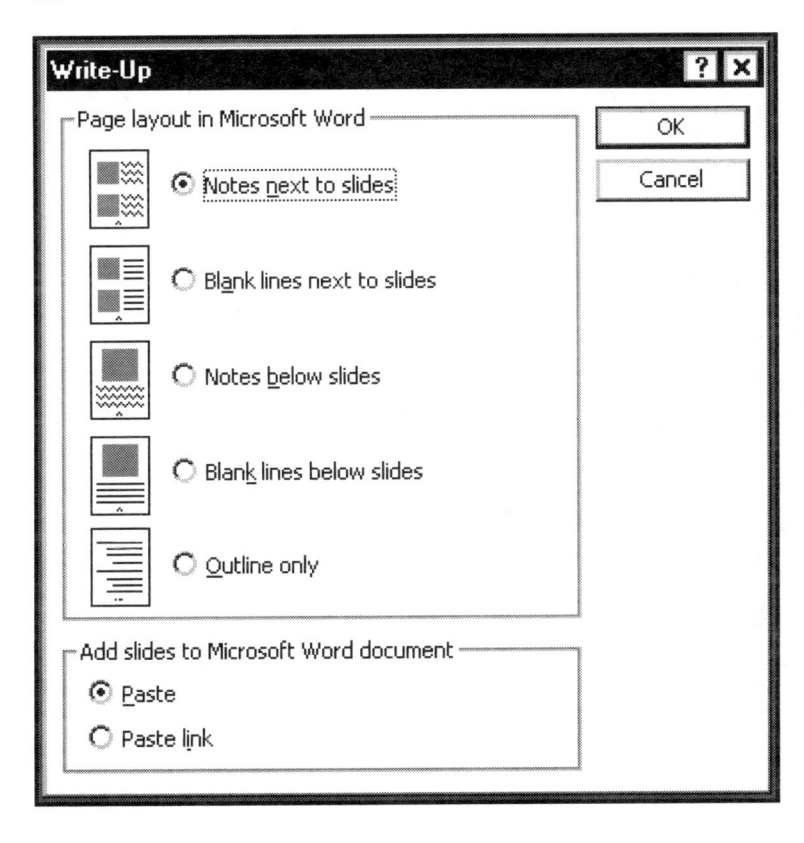

Properties

This displays screens of information about the file (some of which can be edited). The **Statistics** screen is shown for reference.

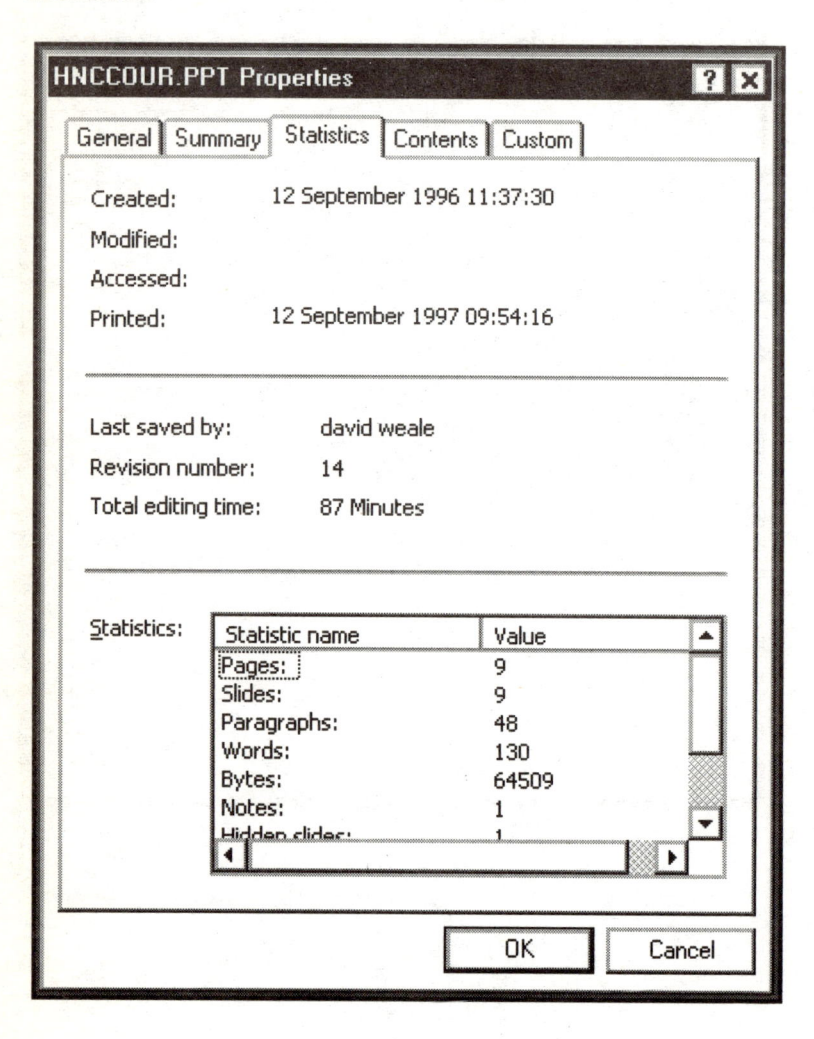

You can also create links to different parts of the slide show by using the **Custom** screen.

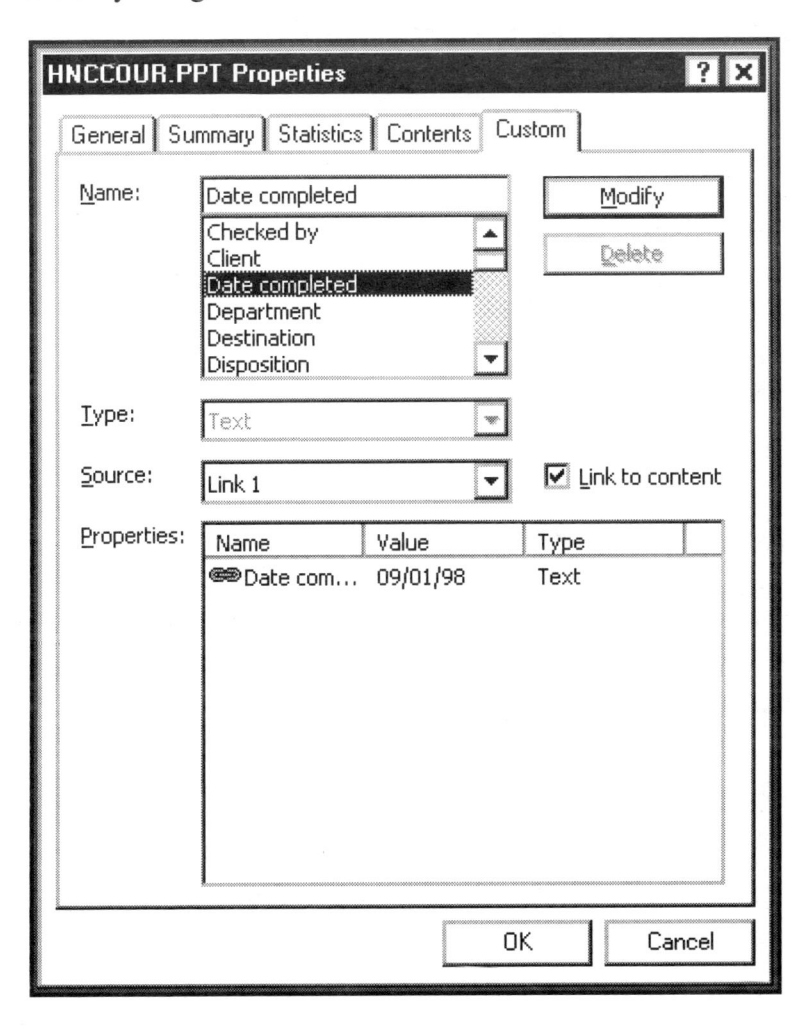

It is necessary to highlight any text or object you want to act as a link before setting up the link. See **Edit** and **Go to Property** for more information.

Edit menu

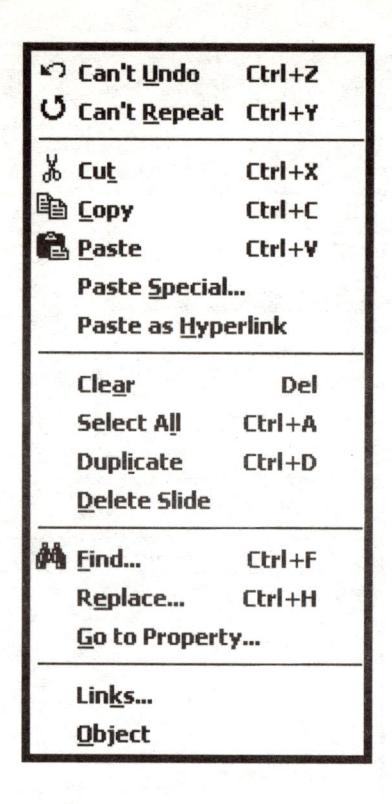

```
↶ Can't Undo        Ctrl+Z
↻ Can't Repeat      Ctrl+Y

✂ Cut               Ctrl+X
📋 Copy             Ctrl+C
📋 Paste            Ctrl+V
   Paste Special...
   Paste as Hyperlink

   Clear            Del
   Select All       Ctrl+A
   Duplicate        Ctrl+D
   Delete Slide

🔍 Find...          Ctrl+F
   Replace...       Ctrl+H
   Go to Property...

   Links...
   Object
```

Cut, Copy and Paste

Remember that you can also **Cut, Copy and Paste** text or images using the appropriate buttons on the toolbar.

Paste Special

This is similar to the Paste command but gives you more control and allows you to create a link to the original application.

If an object is linked, it will be automatically updated when the original is changed.

Paste as Hyperlink

You can copy and paste text or objects as hyperlinks.

For example, you may want to paste a slide title as a hyperlink to that slide, so that if the viewer clicks on the hyperlink then they will jump to that slide.

You can also link to web sites by highlighting the link and clicking on the **Insert Hyperlink** button.

Clear

Selecting this will clear (delete) the selected object or highlighted text.

Select All

This selects all the items (text & objects) on a particular slide **or** if in **Slide Sorter View** will select all the slides.

Duplicate

This allows you to duplicate a slide so that an identical copy is added to the presentation (next to the original). It works using the **Slide Sorter View**, selecting the required slide and then pulling down the **Edit** menu and clicking on **Duplicate**.

Delete Slide

By pulling down the **Edit** menu and choosing **Delete Slide**, you can delete the current slide (or the selected slide(s) in **Slide Sorter View**).

You can also delete a slide in **Slide Sorter View** by selecting the slide(s) and then pressing the **Del** key.

> You can use the **Undo** button if you quickly realise you have deleted the slide(s) accidentally.

Find

A standard text tool, this enables you to find words or parts of words within your presentation. The dialog box is shown below.

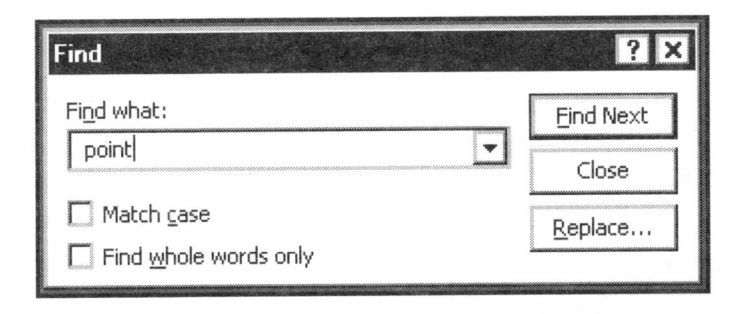

![Find dialog box showing Find what field with "point" entered, Match case and Find whole words only checkboxes, and Find Next, Close, and Replace buttons.]

You enter the word or phrase you are looking for and click on the **Match case** and/or **Find whole words only** if this is what you wish.

Click on the **Find Next** button and the first occurrence of the word will be found and then you can move to the next by clicking on the **Find Next** button and so on.

> You can close down the dialog box and use **Shift** and **F4** to repeat the search.

Replace

Very similar to **Find** except you choose to replace the word or phrase with another as you can see from the dialog box.

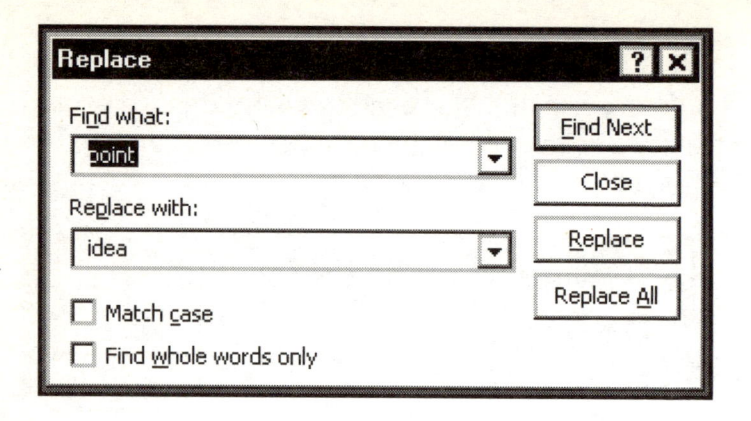

Go to Property

If you set custom properties (**File**, **Properties**) then you can go to the property within the slide using this option.

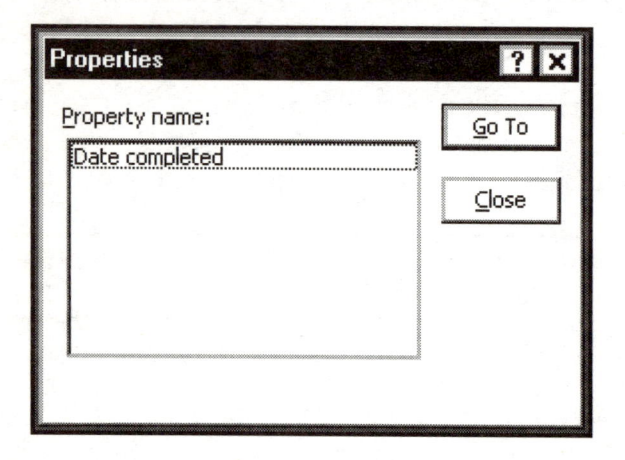

Click on the property and then on **Go To** and it will be displayed.

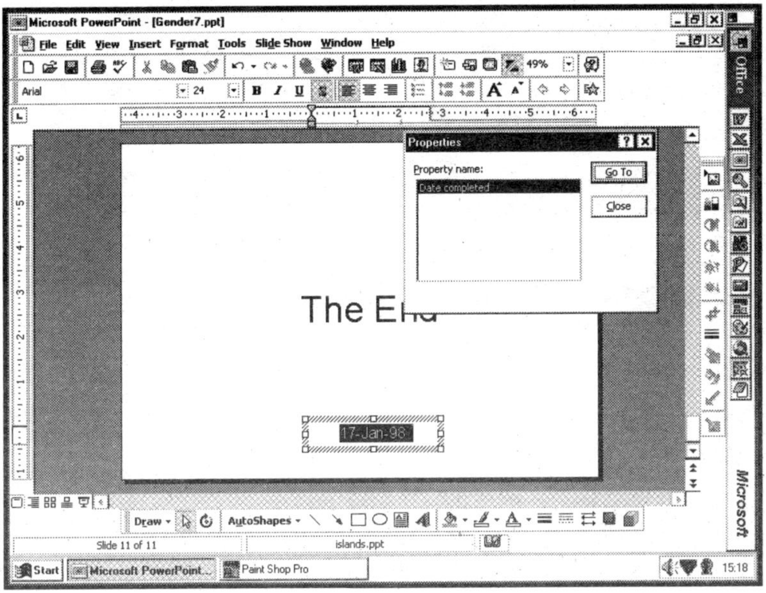
Microsoft PowerPoint - [Gender7.ppt]
File Edit View Insert Format Tools Slide Show Window Help
Arial
24
49%
Properties
Property name:
Date completed
Go To
Close
The End
17-Jan-98
Draw
AutoShapes
Slide 11 of 11
islands.ppt
Start
Microsoft PowerPoint...
Paint Shop Pro
15:18
Office
Microsoft

Links

If you select this option, you will see a dialog box displayed that lets you alter the links.

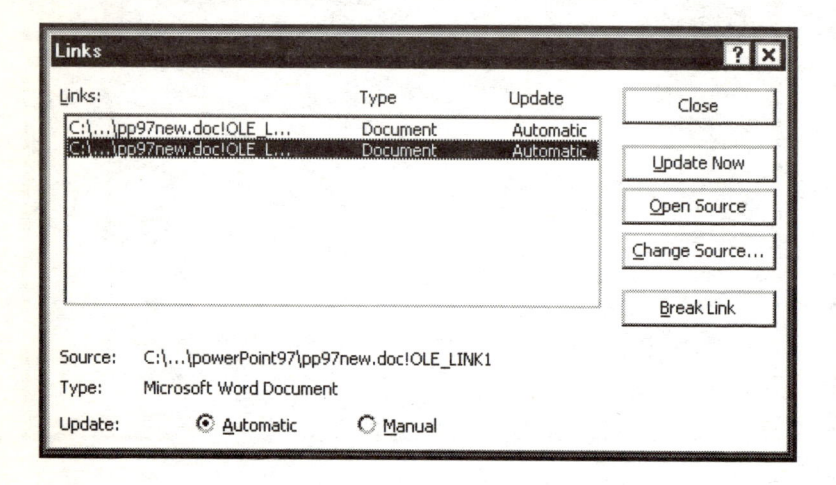

Links:	Type	Update	
C:\...\pp97new.doc!OLE_L...	Document	Automatic	Close
C:\...\pp97new.doc!OLE_L...	Document	Automatic	Update Now
			Open Source
			Change Source...
			Break Link

Source: C:\...\powerPoint97\pp97new.doc!OLE_LINK1
Type: Microsoft Word Document
Update: ● Automatic ○ Manual

This option is not available until you have selected a linked object within your presentation.

Objects

You can edit objects by using the **Edit** menu followed by **Objects** or more quickly by **double clicking** the mouse on the object.

View menu

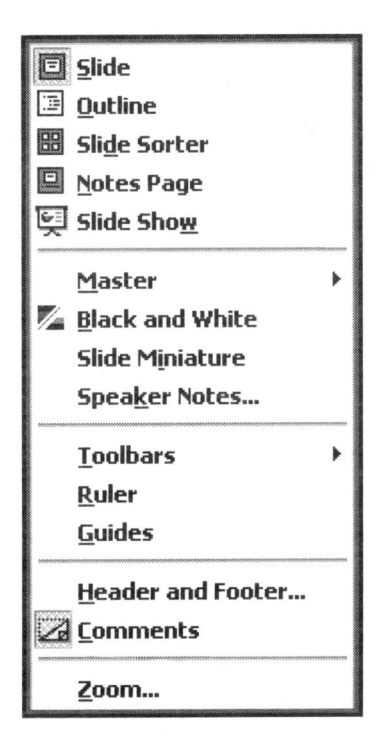

```
Slide
Outline
Slide Sorter
Notes Page
Slide Show

Master         ▶
Black and White
Slide Miniature
Speaker Notes...

Toolbars       ▶
Ruler
Guides

Header and Footer...
Comments

Zoom...
```

Black and White
You can display the slides in black and white.

Slide Miniature
This displays a small (colour) version of the slide in the top right-hand corner of the screen.

Toolbars

You can add or remove any of a number of different toolbars to your screen.

To do this pull down the **View** menu and select **Toolbars**. You will see the dialog box shown below.

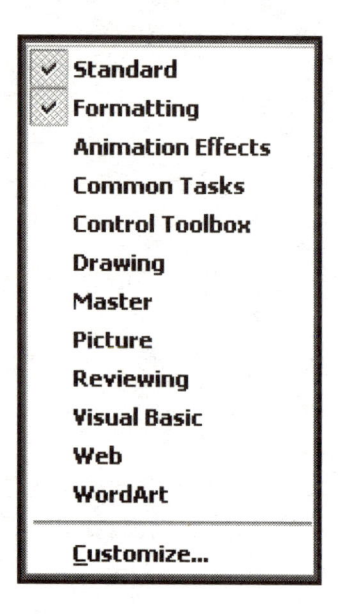

```
✓ Standard
✓ Formatting
  Animation Effects
  Common Tasks
  Control Toolbox
  Drawing
  Master
  Picture
  Reviewing
  Visual Basic
  Web
  WordArt
  ─────────────
  Customize...
```

By selecting or deselecting the different toolbars you can add (or remove) them.

You can select a toolbar on the screen by double clicking on it, you can then move it around the screen to a new position.

Once a toolbar has been selected, you can change the shape by moving the mouse pointer along an edge until it becomes a two headed arrow that can then be dragged to produce a new shape.

Rulers

You can display the rulers by selecting this option.

Guides

You can display or hide the guides by using the **View** menu and then **Guides**.

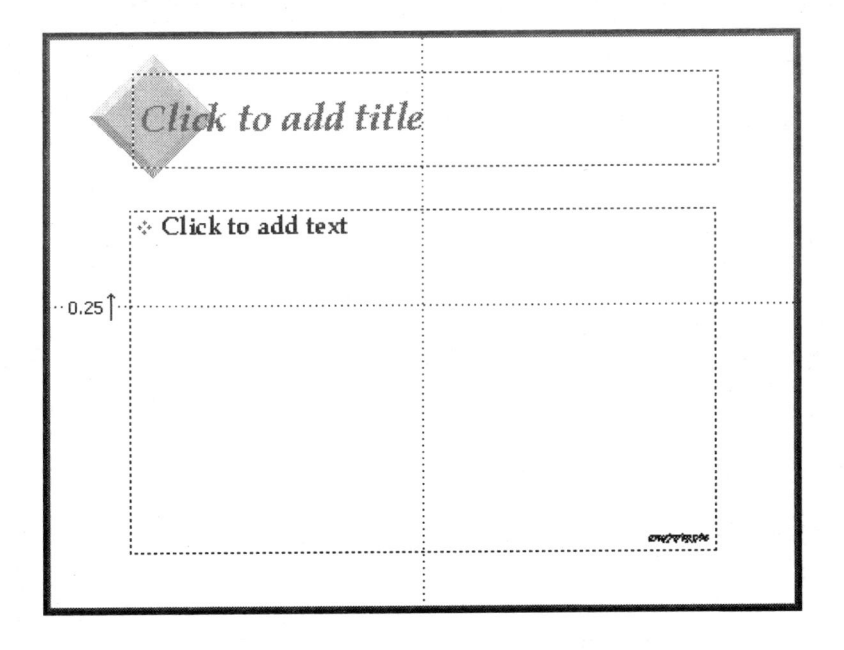

Guides are useful to position objects or text and they can be moved horizontally or vertically by clicking the mouse pointer on the guide and dragging it.

Headers and Footers

You can insert the date and time, slide numbers and footers (you type in the text you want) using this feature.

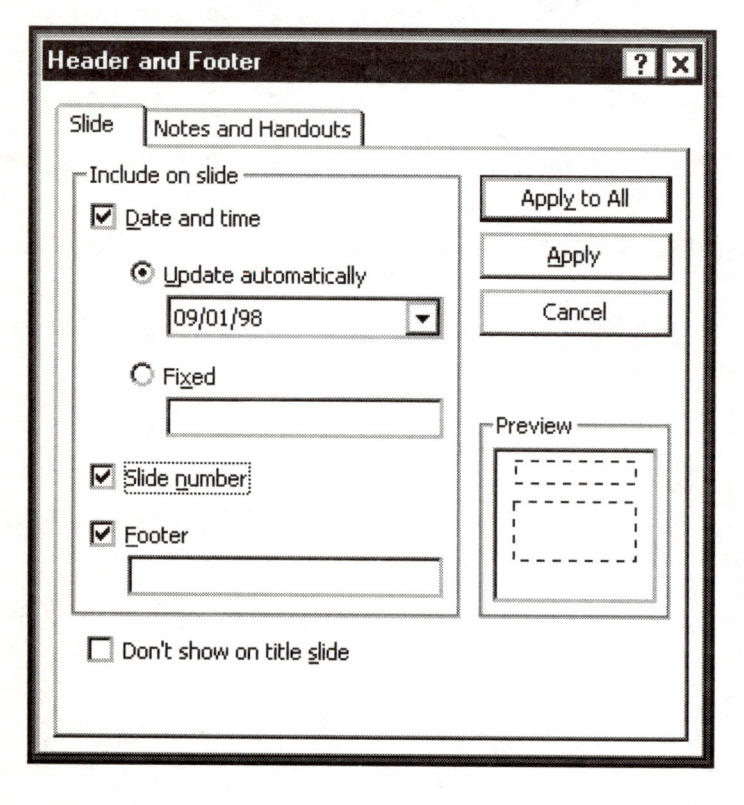

The **Notes and Handouts** option lets you do the same for the notes and handout pages.

You can see how footers appear from the illustration.

> Click to add title
>
> Click to add sub-title
>
> 09/01/98   first presentation   1

Comments

This displays the comments you have added to the slide (or hides the comments).

You need to have inserted the comments (**Insert** followed by **Comments**).

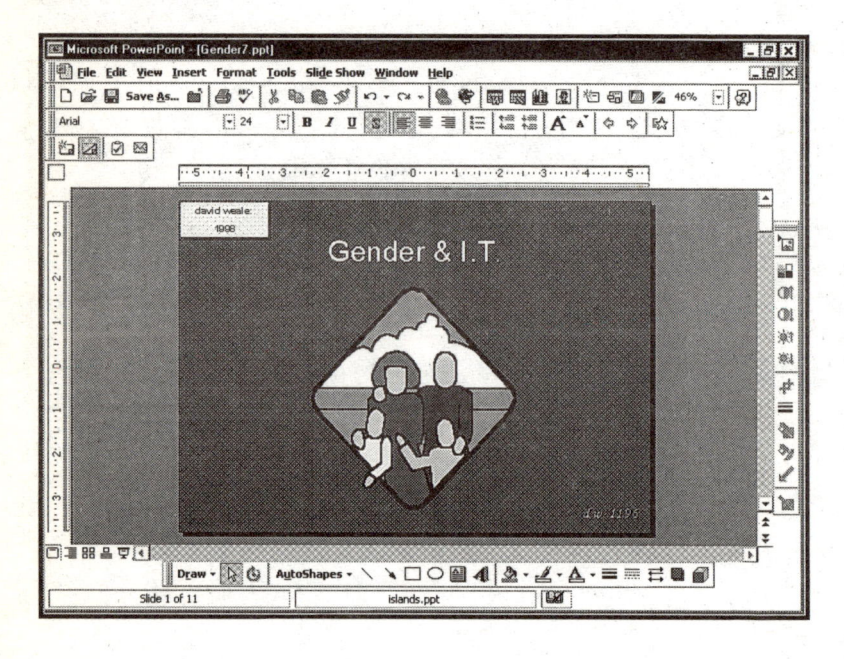

Insert menu

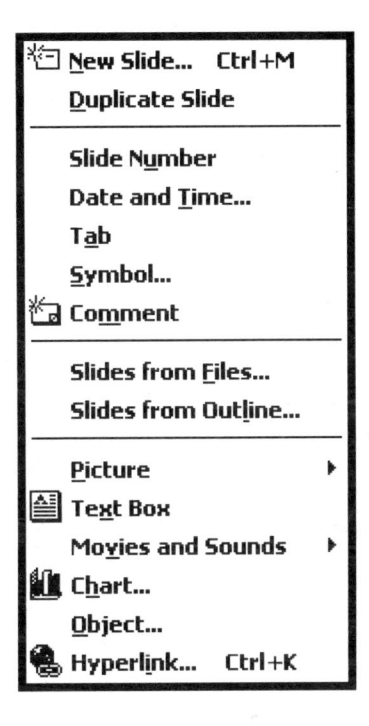

```
New Slide...   Ctrl+M
Duplicate Slide

Slide Number
Date and Time...
Tab
Symbol...
Comment

Slides from Files...
Slides from Outline...

Picture              ▶
Text Box
Movies and Sounds    ▶
Chart...
Object...
Hyperlink...   Ctrl+K
```

Duplicate Slide

This creates a copy the current slide and inserts it into the slide show. Useful if you are making minor alterations to the slide.

Slide Number / Date and Time

Normally you would use the **Header and Footer** command (**View** menu) to insert page numbers and dates on the **Master** slide.

However, if you want to insert page numbers or dates on individual slides, you can use this feature. Remember you need to create a text box to do so.

Tab

A way of inserting variable **tab** stops into text. If you use the **TAB** key, you will get the default half-inch tabs.

Remember that using the **TAB** key at the start of a line of text will demote that line so it becomes a subheading (see **Outlines**).

Comment

You can insert comments onto your slides, simply select this option and type in the comment you want to make. You can hide or display the comments using the **View** menu.

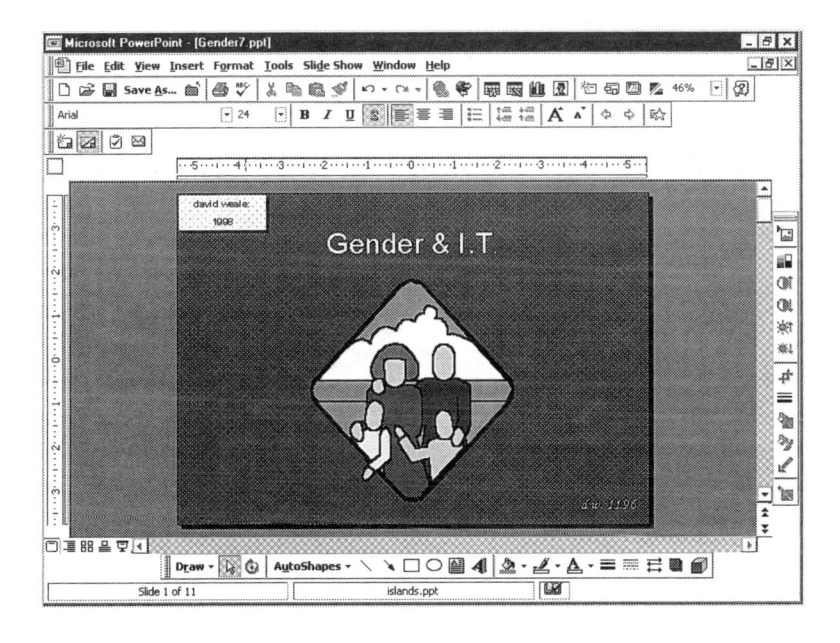

Slides from Files

This option lets you add slides from another file into your current presentation.

To do this, pull down the **Insert** menu and select **Slides from File**. You will see a dialog box similar to the Open File dialog box and you simply select the file you want to add.

Note that the new slides will be added after the current slide, and the other slides in the original presentation will be re-sequenced.

> You may find it best to use **Slide Sorter View** and position the cursor where you want the new slides to be added.

Slides from Outline

This is slightly different in that PowerPoint will automatically create a slide show from an outline, using the outline levels as a guide, the first level text is treated as a heading and so on.

For example if you either created an outline within **Word** or used an outline from an existing file then you could use this to create a PowerPoint presentation without having to retype the text. This works rather effectively and is a real time-saver.

To do this, pull down the **Insert** menu and select **Slides from Outline**. Find the file you want to use and PowerPoint will convert it into a presentation. You will then need to make any alterations and to customise the presentation.

Pictures

These are treated in a very similar way to clipart, they can (mostly but not always, depending upon the type of file) be sized, recoloured, grouped and ungrouped and so on.

Scanned images require a large amount of disc space to store and tend to slow the system up when used.

A partial fix for this is to scale the scanned image before saving it so that it is the correct size.

However, you should not make it too small as increasing the size of an image can reduce the definition.

To insert a picture (that is not in the Microsoft Clip Gallery), pull down the **Insert** menu and select **Picture** and then **From File**.

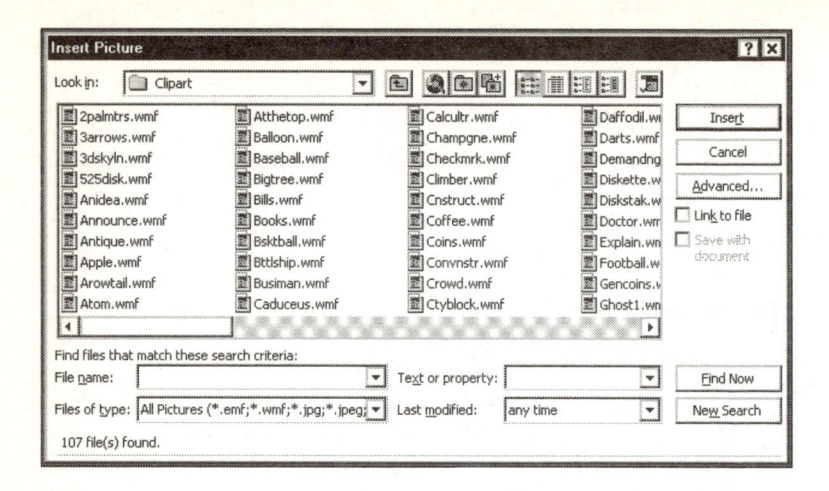

Find the picture on your hard disc and **Insert** it into your presentation.

The screen below shows a picture imported in this way.

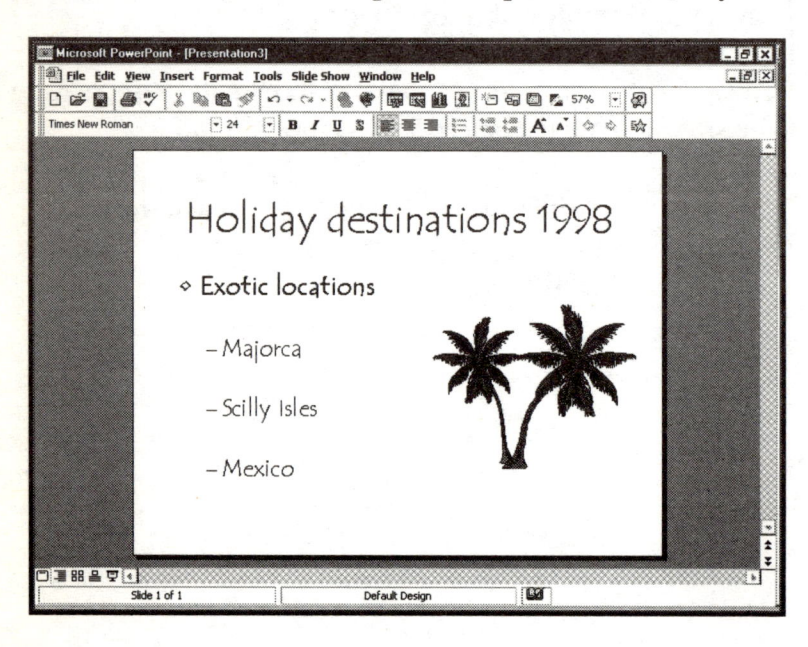

Text Box

You can insert a text box anywhere in a slide by selecting this option and then dragging the mouse to create the box, into which you type the text you want.

Movies and Sounds

Use this option to insert movie clips and sounds that may not have been installed into the **Microsoft Clip Gallery**. You will see a menu of choices (Gallery refers to the Clip Gallery).

```
Movie from Gallery...
Movie from File...

Sound from Gallery...
Sound from File...
Play CD Audio Track...
Record Sound
```

If you insert a movie then you will see an image that you can click to activate the movie when you view the slide show.

Microsoft PowerPoint - [Presentation1]
File Edit View Insert Format Tools Slide Show Window Help
Save As...
46%
Office
Draw
AutoShapes
Slide 1 of 1
Default Design
Microsoft
Start
STB Vision 95 Con...
Microsoft Word - p...
Microsoft Powe...
Paint Shop Pro
16:54

Similarly with sounds.

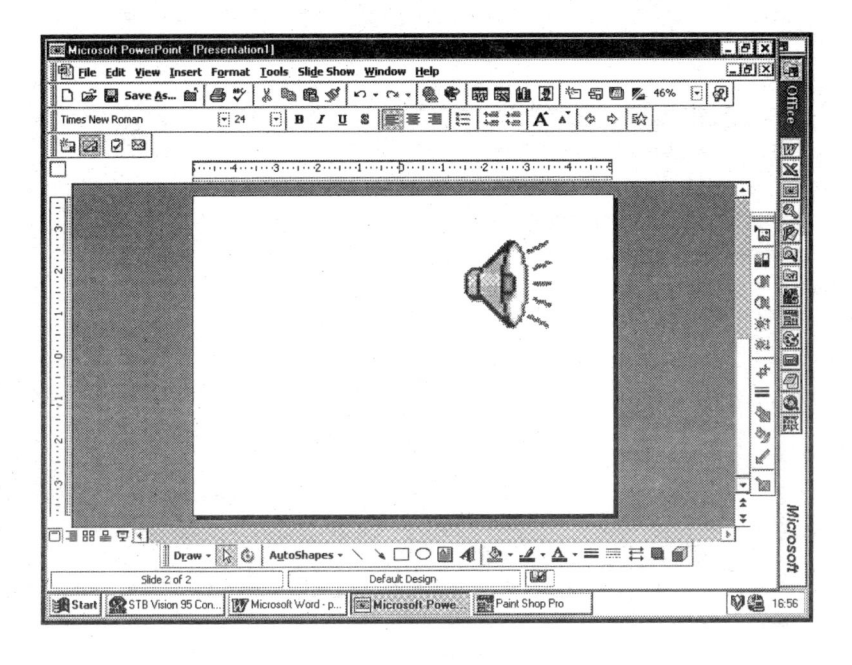

You can alter the way in which the movie or sound appears by using the **Slide Show** menu followed by **Custom Animation**.

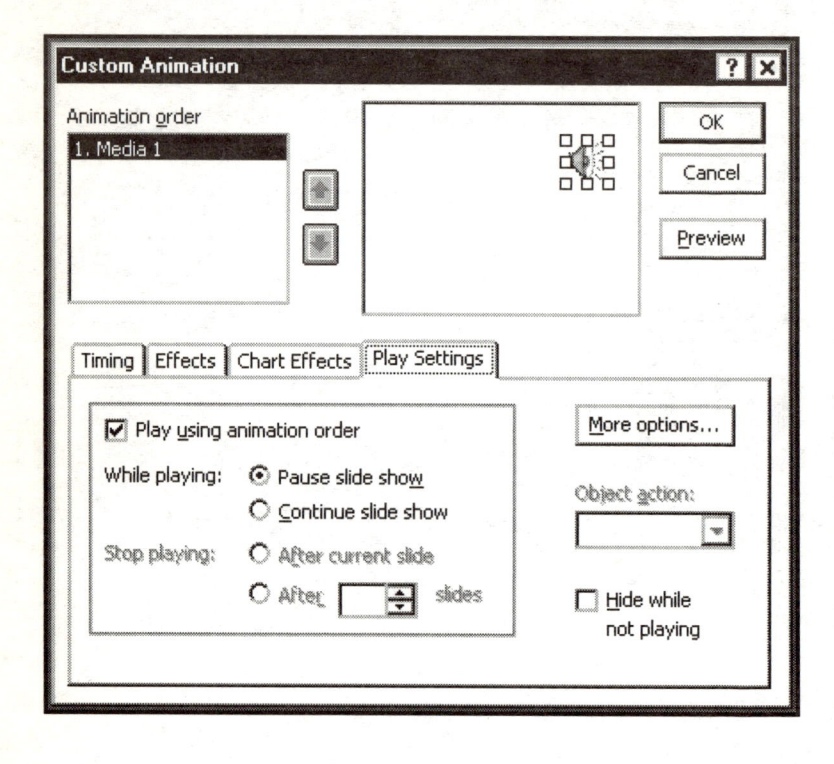

Format menu

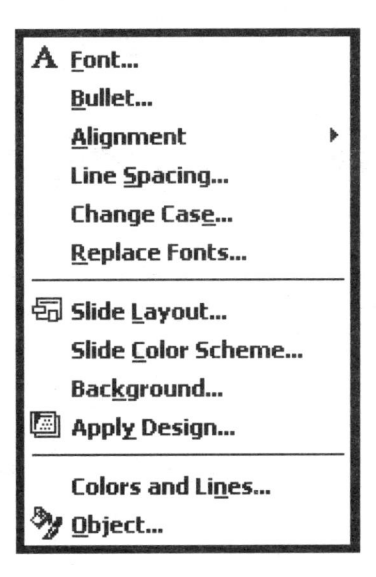

- A **F**ont...
- **B**ullet...
- **A**lignment ▶
- Line **S**pacing...
- Change Cas**e**...
- **R**eplace Fonts...

- Slide **L**ayout...
- Slide **C**olor Scheme...
- Bac**k**ground...
- Appl**y** Design...

- Colors and Li**n**es...
- **O**bject...

Font

You can alter the font by using the toolbar button, however you have more flexibility by pulling down the **Format** menu and then **Font**.

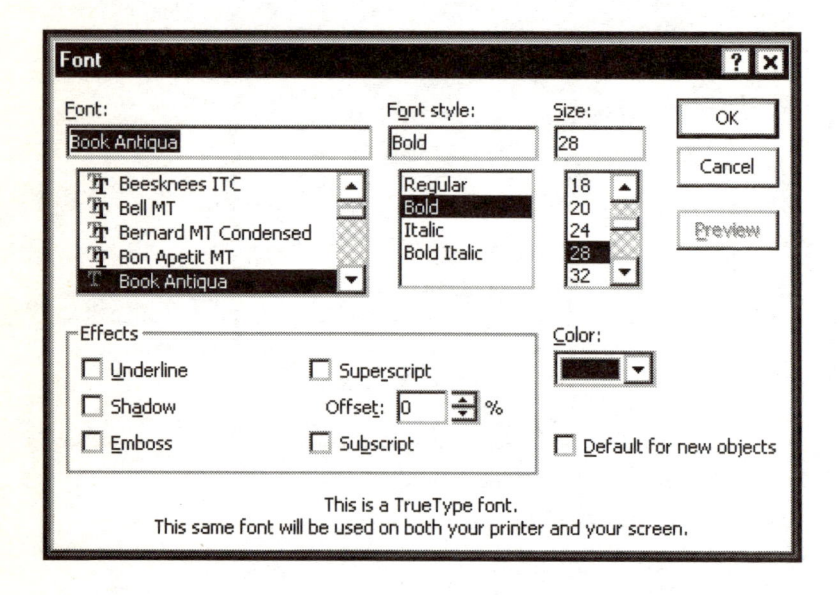

Changing the Text Colour

Although a design will automatically use its own colour scheme, you can alter the text colour easily.

Select the text to be changed by highlighting. Click on the **Format** menu and **Font**, then click on the **Color** box and select a different colour.

> You can highlight any character or characters and alter its colour irrespective of the remainder of the text.

Changing the Bullets

If you want to alter the predefined bullets (again you can make these changes for an individual slide or for all the slides by altering the **Master Slide**), firstly select the text for which you want to alter the bullets and then pull down the **Format** menu and select **Bullets**.

There are various options. You can choose bullets from any character set you have installed and you can alter the colour of the bullet and/or its relative size.

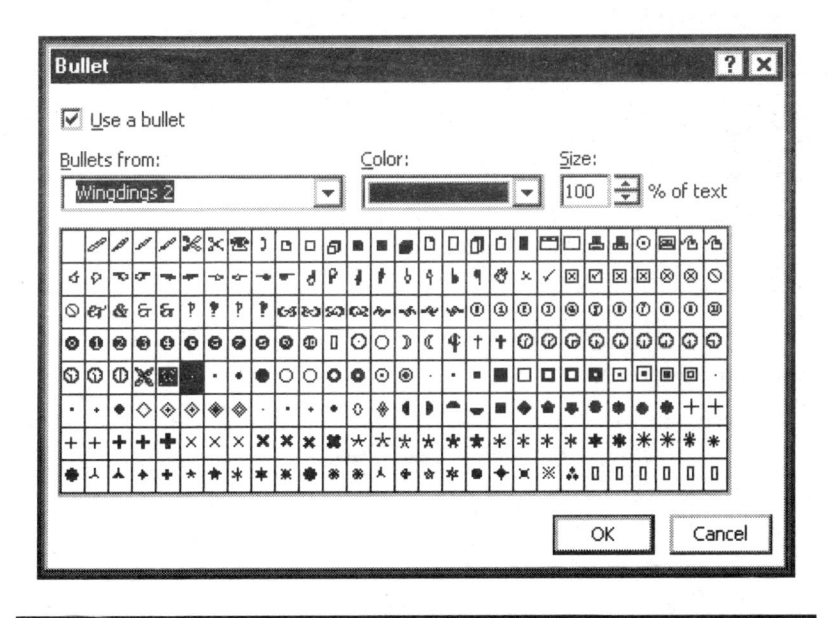

You can remove bullets by clicking on the **Use a Bullet** box so that there is not an **X** in it (after selecting the text).

Alignment

To alter the alignment of a paragraph (or more), highlight the text and then either pull down the **Format** menu and select **Alignment** or use the alignment buttons on the toolbar. The Alignment menu gives more choice.

Alternatively, you can use the following keys (holding the first down while depressing the latter).

CTRL E	centre
CTRL J	justify
CTRL L	left
CTRL R	right

Line Spacing

Obviously hitting the **Return** key will create space, unfortunately it will also create another bullet. To avoid this, hold down the **Shift** key while depressing the **Return** key, this is a soft return and does not give rise to a new bullet. This is a crude method however and the most satisfactory method to alter the line spacing, whether for an individual slide or for the master slide is to use the **Format** menu and then **Line Spacing**.

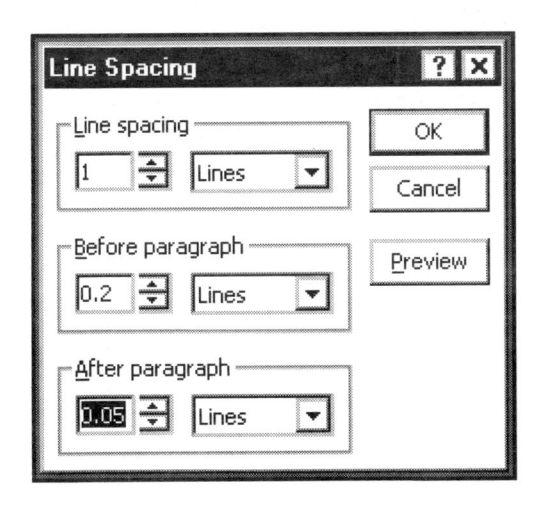

A dialog box will appear and you can alter the line spacing and the space before and after paragraphs as you wish. Better still, you will be able to see the effect on screen as you make the changes.

You **must** highlight the text to alter the line spacing in this version of the program.

Grab the dialog box and move it out of the way so that you can see the effect more clearly when you **Preview**.

Change Case

You can change the case of the text you have typed in. Believe me this is very useful, it is very easy to type text with the **Caps Lock** key on by mistake.

To use this feature you need to highlight the text and then pull down the **Format** menu and select **Change Case**. Then choose how you want to alter the text.

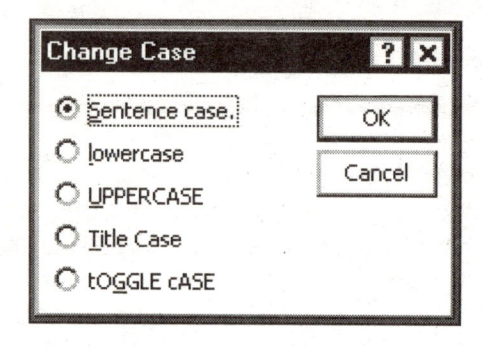

You can also use **Shift** and **F3** to alter the case of highlighted text.

Replacing Fonts

In the **Format** menu is an option called **Replace Fonts**. This lets you alter one font to another, so that all type in that font is altered to the new font.

The dialog box is shown below, you can use the arrows to the right of each box to alter the choices.

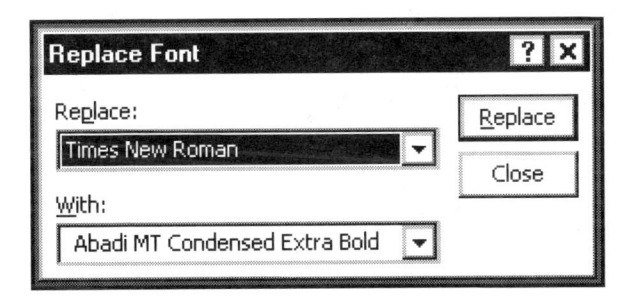

Slide Colour Scheme

You can alter the standard colour scheme or go into **Custom** and alter the scheme as you wish.

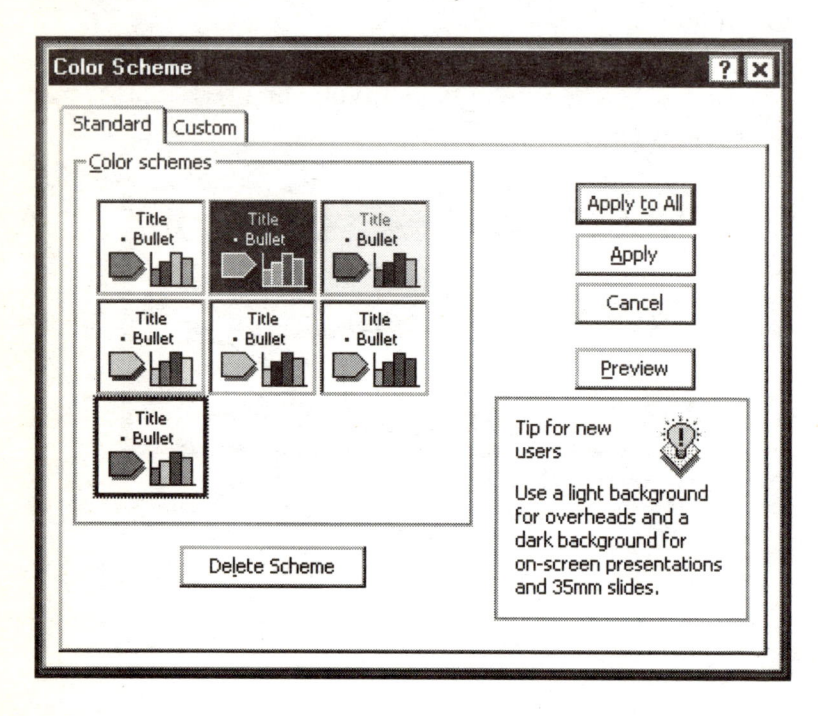

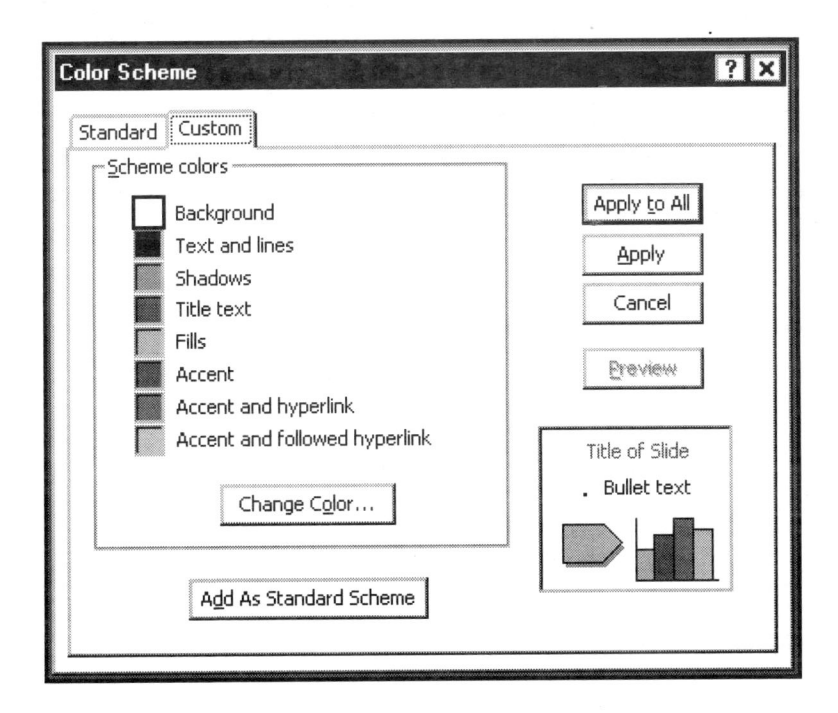

You can add any custom colour scheme you create to the standard schemes.

Background

Pull down the **Format** menu and select **Slide Background**. You will see the following dialog box. Choose another colour and **Preview** or **Apply** it to your slides.

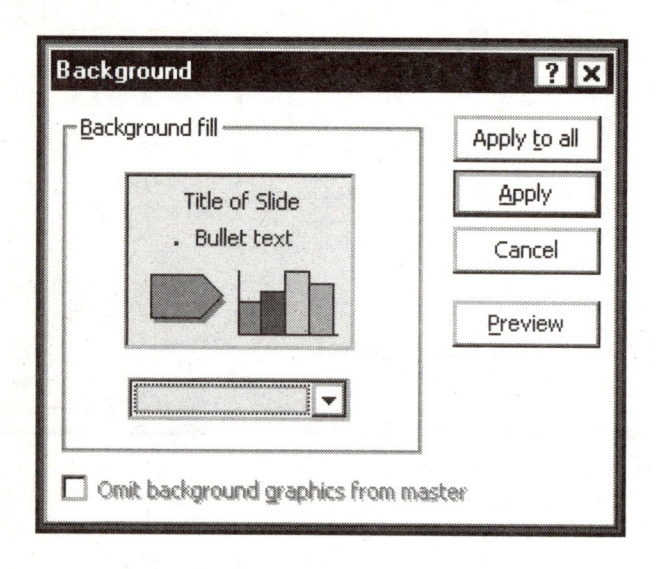

Be careful with the buttons **Apply To All** and **Apply**. Your choice will depend upon whether you want to change the background of all the slides or not.

Colour and Lines

You can add borders and fills to text boxes or objects.

Click on the object or text so that the text box or object boundaries are shown (you should see little squares positioned around the border).

Then pull down the **Format** menu and select **Colours & Lines**. Choose the colour and thickness of the line or fill and so on.

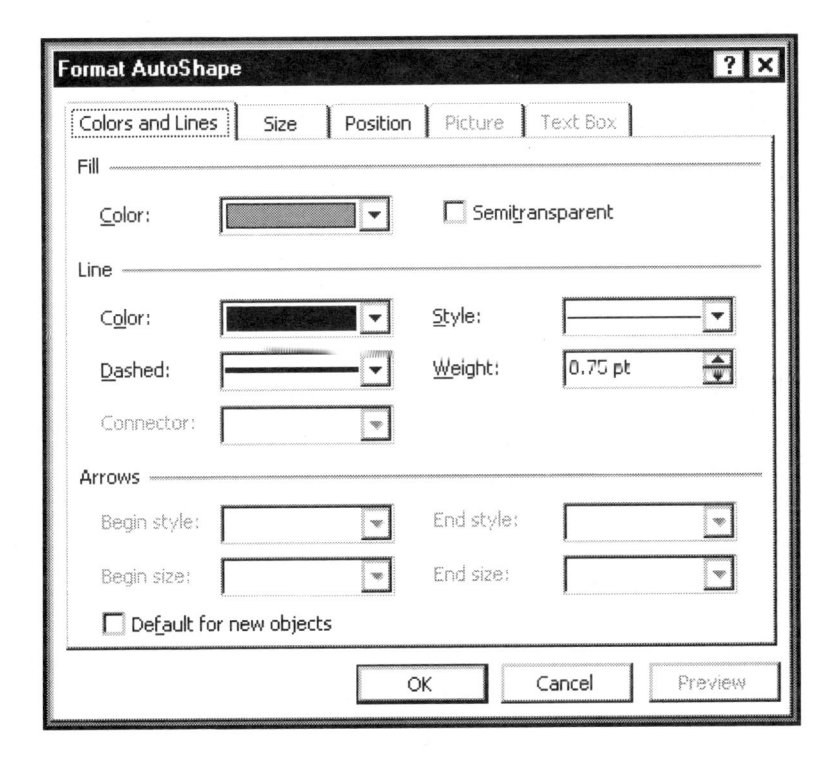

Object / Picture

Once you have selected an object or picture, you can alter the look of it by using the various tools within this dialog box.

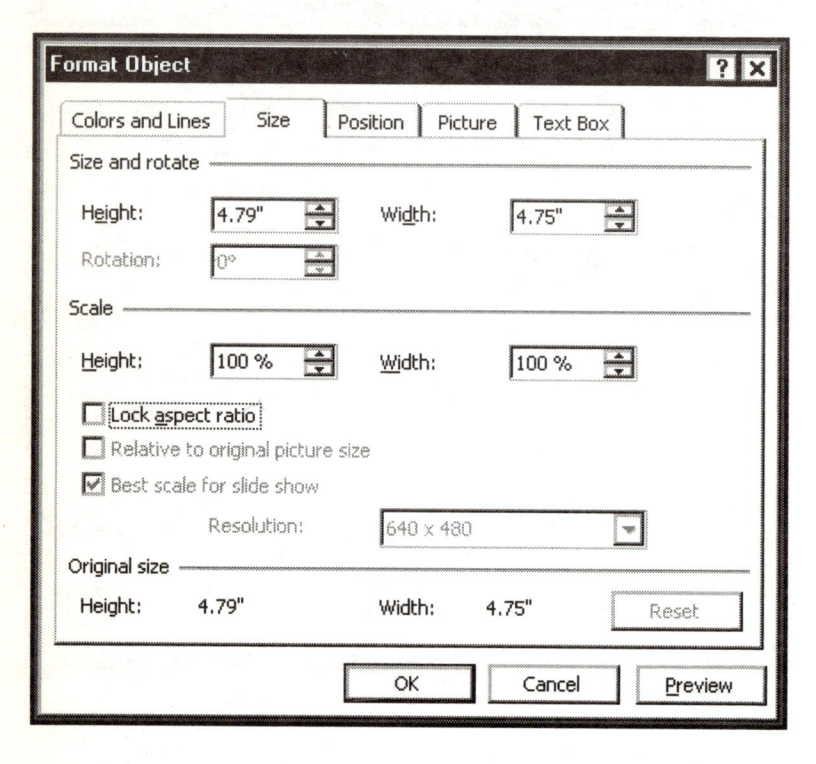

Of especial importance is whether you want the image to **Float over text** (see illustration on the next page). This is the default and allows you to position the image wherever you want (in a similar way to frames available in previous versions of the program).

If you want to align the image (e.g. centre it) then you need to remove the tick to the left of **Float over text**. Note that this option is only available with certain images.

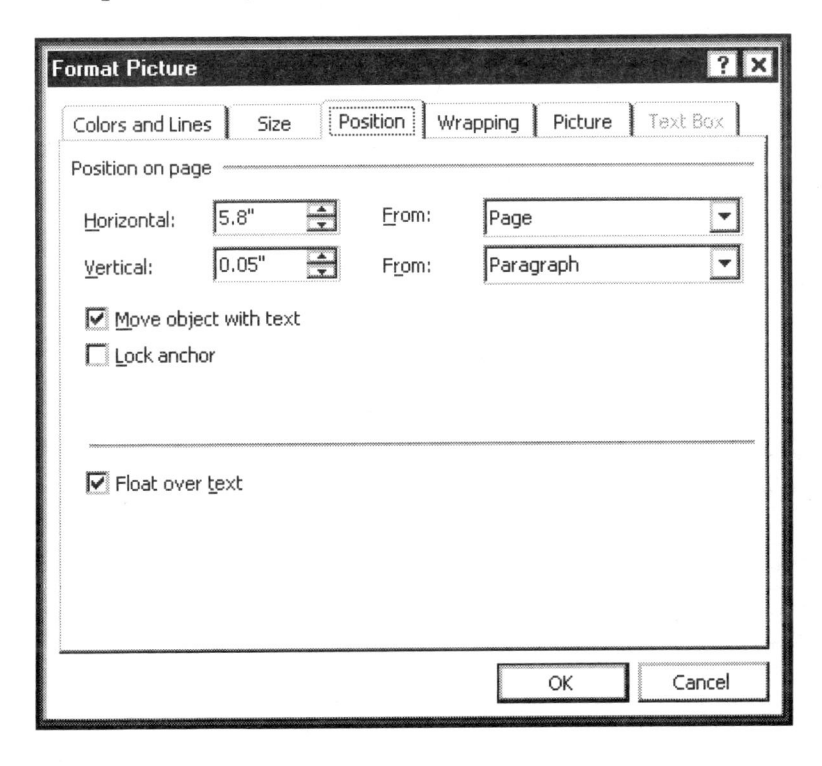

Format Painter

This button allows you to quickly alter how any object appears by copying the attributes (colour, shading, etc.) from another object (it may not work with graphs or pictures).

To work with the **Format Painter**, click on the object you want to copy the formatting **from**, then click on the Format Painter button and then click on the object you want to copy the attributes to.

Tools menu

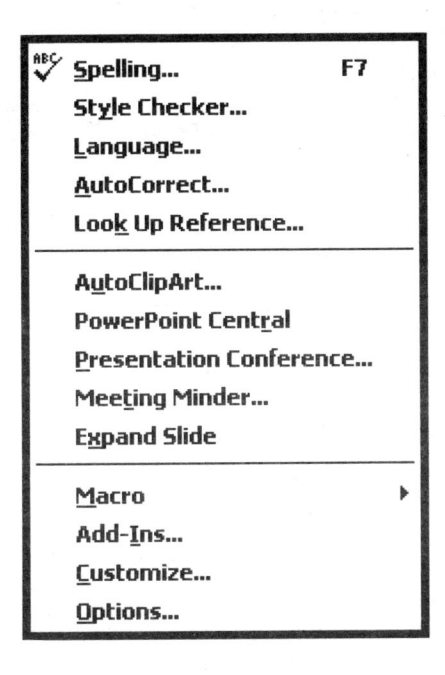

✓ **S**pelling...	F7
St**y**le Checker...	
Language...	
AutoCorrect...	
Loo**k** Up Reference...	

A**u**toClipArt...
PowerPoint Cent**r**al
Presentation Conference...
Mee**t**ing Minder...
E**x**pand Slide

Macro ▶
Add-**I**ns...
Customize...
Options...

Style Checker

This checks the consistency and correctness of your slides; spelling, grammar and formatting are checked.

You can set your own options by clicking on the **Options** button and altering the settings.

An example of the reports you get is shown.

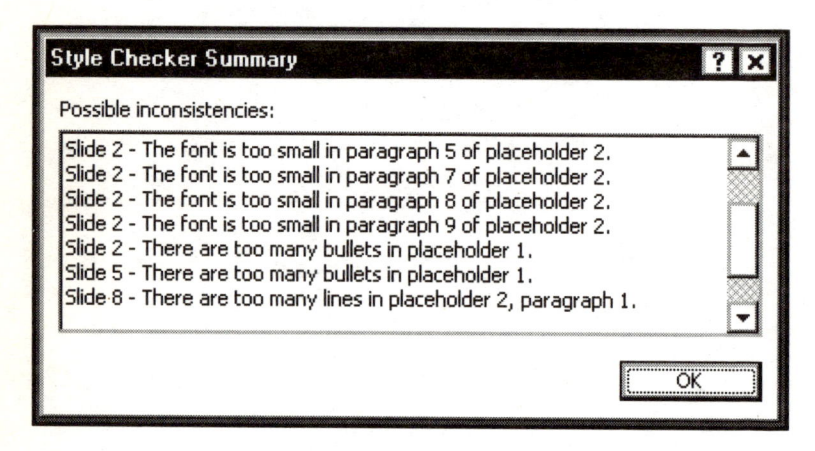

Language

You use this to set the language (for spelling and other checking purposes). The default is the choice of language you made when you installed Windows (to alter the default use the **Control Panel**).

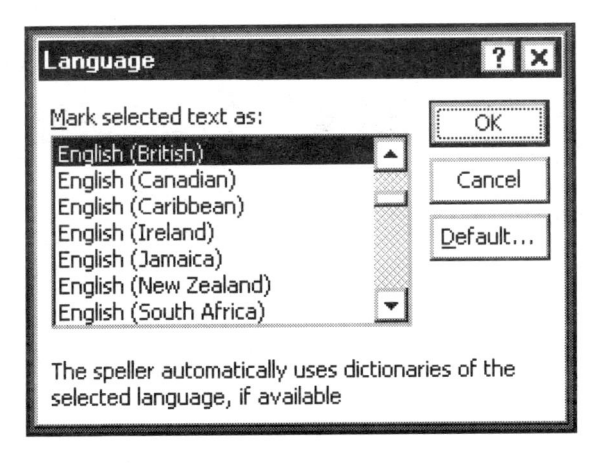

AutoCorrect

This sets various rules for the **AutoCorrect** feature. You can make any alterations you want, delete rules, add new rules, and create exceptions to the rules and so on.

To turn off this feature simply click the **Replace text as you type** so that there is no tick in the box.

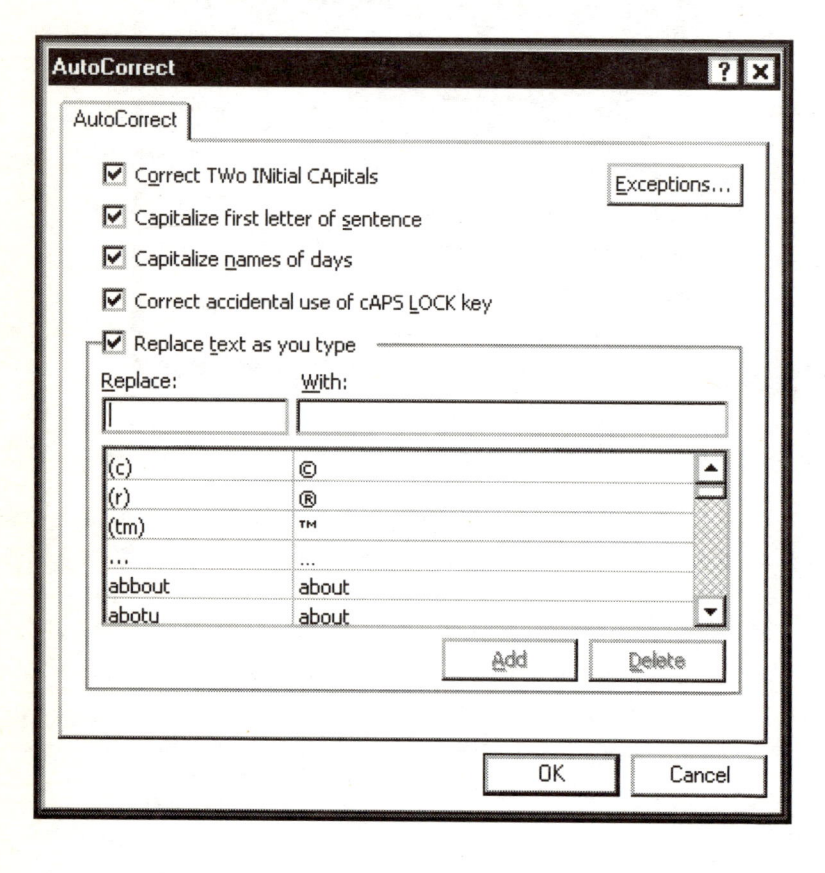

Look Up Reference

This lets you search certain (installed) reference tools. The reference is loaded automatically once you have clicked the **OK** button.

You can speed the search process by choosing how you want to search and what words you want to search for.

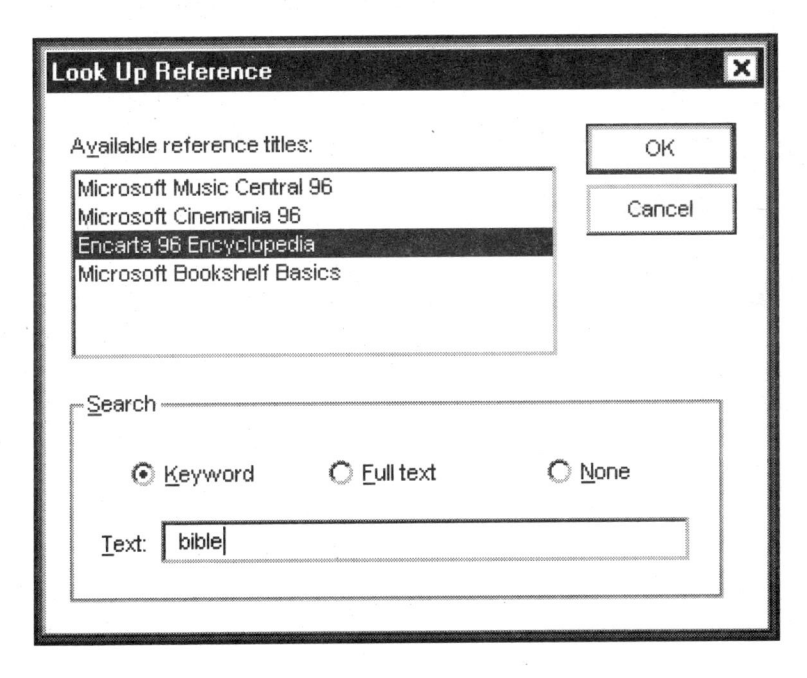

AutoClipArt

You can use this feature to find relevant clipart, sounds, etc., for your slide(s). From the dialog box you select a word and then the Microsoft Clip Gallery is loaded with the relevant items displayed.

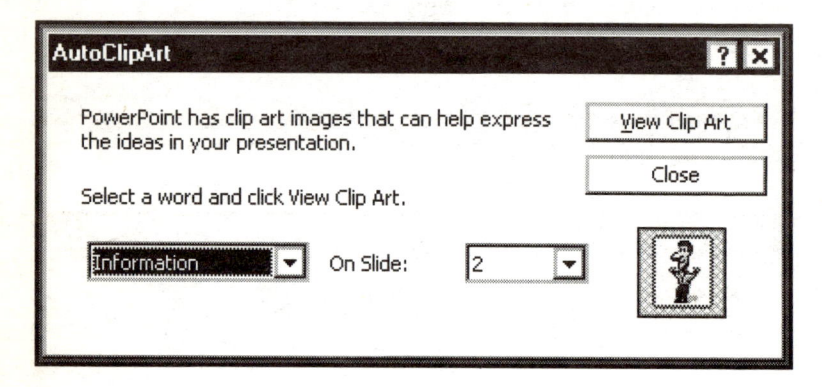

PowerPoint Central

To use this feature you need to be connected to the Internet. It downloads the latest features of PowerPoint onto your hard disc. There are many useful tips and enhancements available from Microsoft and this is a quick and easy way of obtaining them.

When you select this feature, you will connect to the Microsoft site and the initial screen you will see will look similar to this.

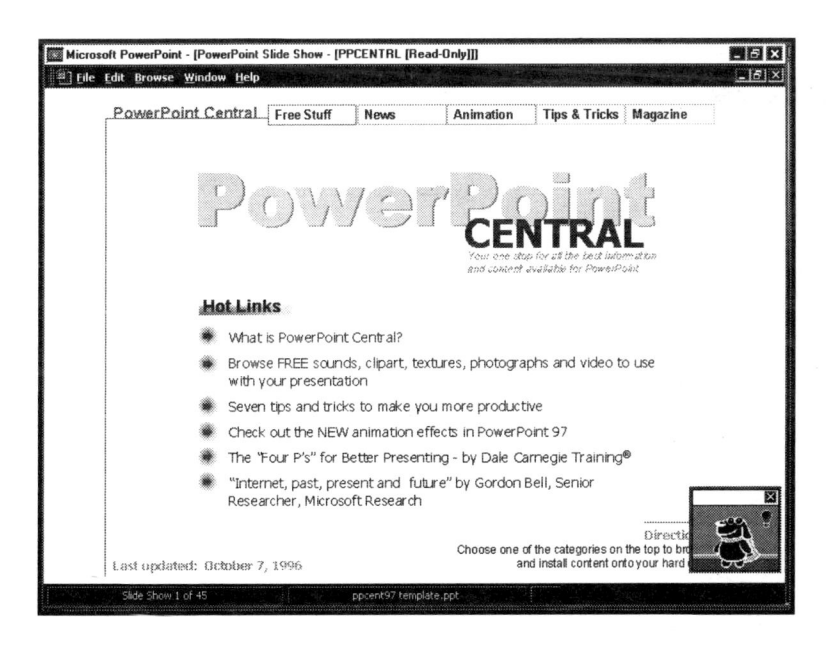

Presentation Conference
You can use this to participate in a presentation across a network, an Intranet or the Internet. A Wizard takes you through the various steps.

Expand Slide
This takes the main points on a slide and creates a new slide for each point.

Macro
A macro (in its simplest form) is a series of commands, keystrokes and other activities. You record this series and you can then play it back without having to enter the keystrokes individually.

Add-Ins
These are additional programs, which enhance the use of PowerPoint. You can obtain add-in programs from a variety of sources.

Customise

This enables you to add and delete buttons to reflect the way you personally work.

After pulling down the **Tools** menu, select **Customise** and you will see a dialog box.

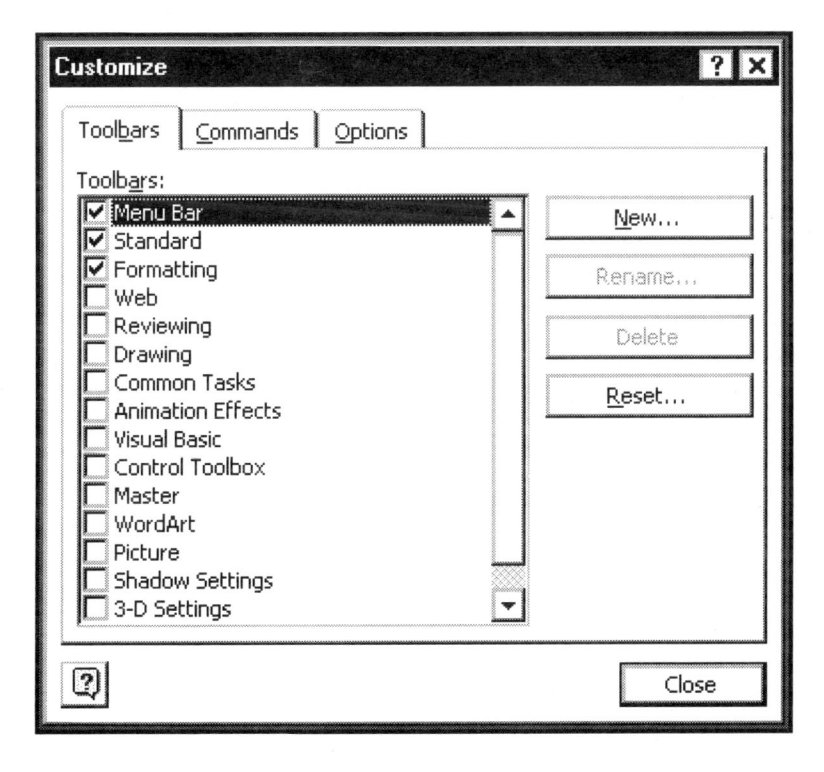

![Customize dialog box showing Toolbars tab with list of toolbars including Menu Bar, Standard, Formatting, Web, Reviewing, Drawing, Common Tasks, Animation Effects, Visual Basic, Control Toolbox, Master, WordArt, Picture, Shadow Settings, 3-D Settings, and buttons for New, Rename, Delete, Reset, Close]

You can select from the different toolbars shown.

You can add buttons (for that toolbar) by selecting the **Commands** tab and then grabbing the button and dragging it to **any** toolbar on the screen.

143

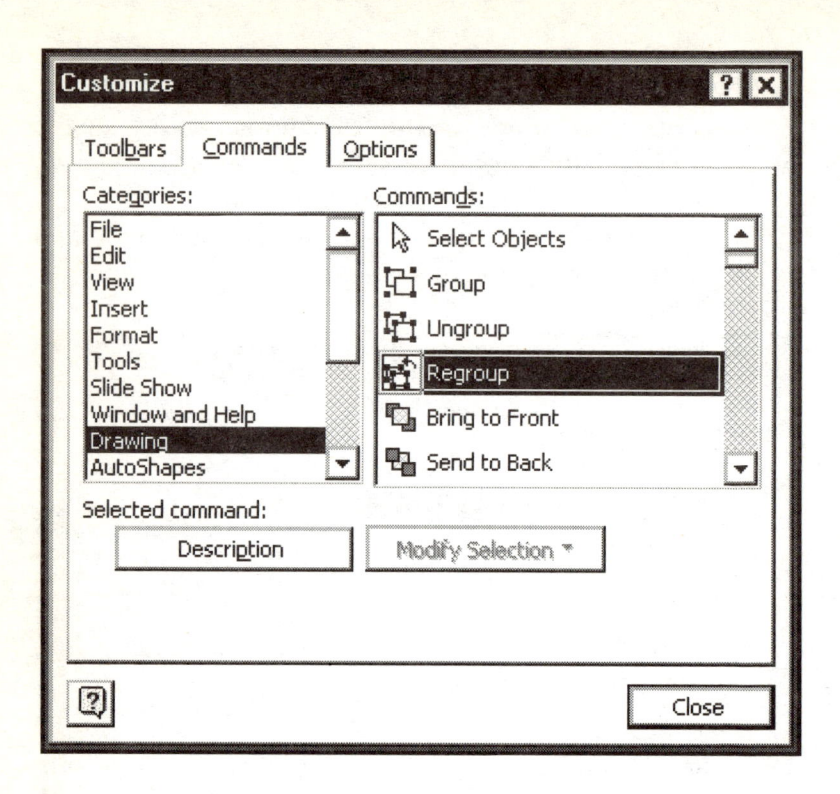

To remove a button, simply drag it off the toolbar.

> If you decide that you have made a mess of any toolbar then the **Reset** button on the **Toolbar** menu lets you put everything back to its default position.

Options

In addition, in the **Tools** menu is **Options**. This is where you can make various changes to the way the program works.

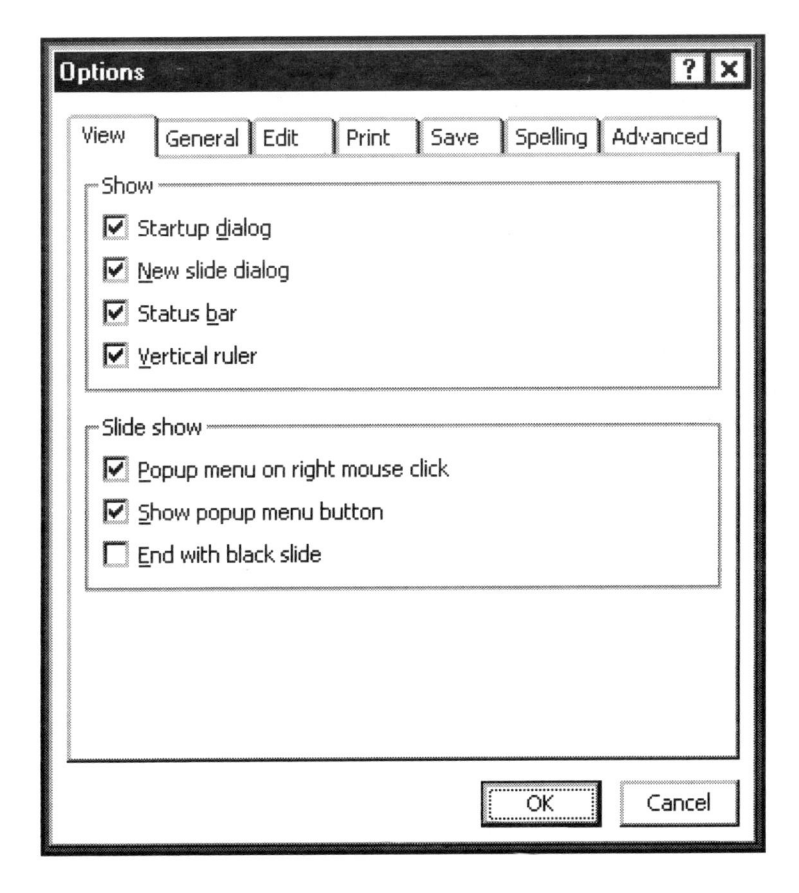

```
Options                                              ? X
┌──────────────────────────────────────────────────────┐
│ View │ General │ Edit │ Print │ Save │ Spelling │ Advanced │
│ ┌─Show─────────────────────────────────────────────┐ │
│ │  ☑ Startup dialog                                │ │
│ │  ☑ New slide dialog                              │ │
│ │  ☑ Status bar                                    │ │
│ │  ☑ Vertical ruler                                │ │
│ └──────────────────────────────────────────────────┘ │
│ ┌─Slide show───────────────────────────────────────┐ │
│ │  ☑ Popup menu on right mouse click               │ │
│ │  ☑ Show popup menu button                        │ │
│ │  ☐ End with black slide                          │ │
│ └──────────────────────────────────────────────────┘ │
│                                                      │
│                                    [ OK ]  [ Cancel ]│
└──────────────────────────────────────────────────────┘
```

Each of the tabs (**View**, **General**, **Edit**, etc.) contains program settings that you can alter from the default. Some are explained below.

Replace Straight Quotes with Smart Quotes
Replaces ordinary quotes (straight quotes) with curly ones which you may prefer.

Automatic Word Selection
When you use the mouse to select text, the text is highlighted in groups of words, if this feature is turned off then you will be able to select partial words or individual characters.

Smart Cut and Paste
Makes a space between words when the Clipboard contents are pasted into your slides.

Slide Show Menu

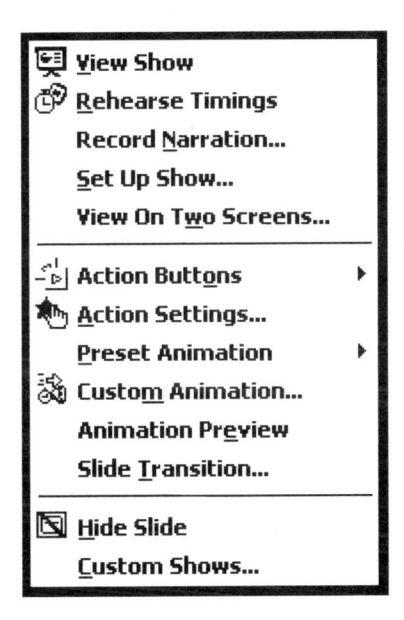

```
View Show
Rehearse Timings
Record Narration...
Set Up Show...
View On Two Screens...

Action Buttons         ▶
Action Settings...
Preset Animation       ▶
Custom Animation...
Animation Preview
Slide Transition...

Hide Slide
Custom Shows...
```

View Show

This runs the slide show, you can use the **Slide Show** button instead.

Rehearse Timings

This runs the slide show, rehearsing the timings you have set **or** you can set timings using this option.

To set timings using the **Rehearse Timings** option, simply use the dialog box (shown below).

You can use the arrow symbol to advance the slides and the **Repeat** and **Pause** buttons as appropriate. When you have finished, you will be asked if you want to save the new timings.

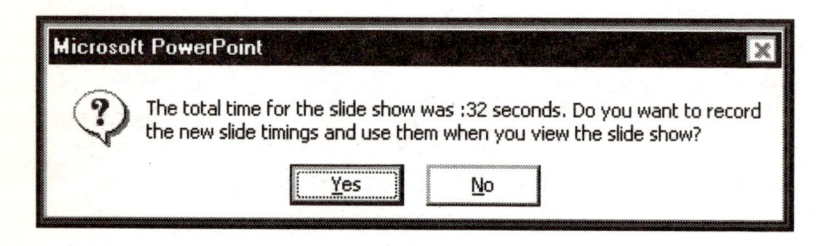

Record Narration

If you have the necessary sound card and microphone then you can add a spoken commentary to your slide show. This can be done while you are doing the presentation (with audience participation if you wish) or at some other time.

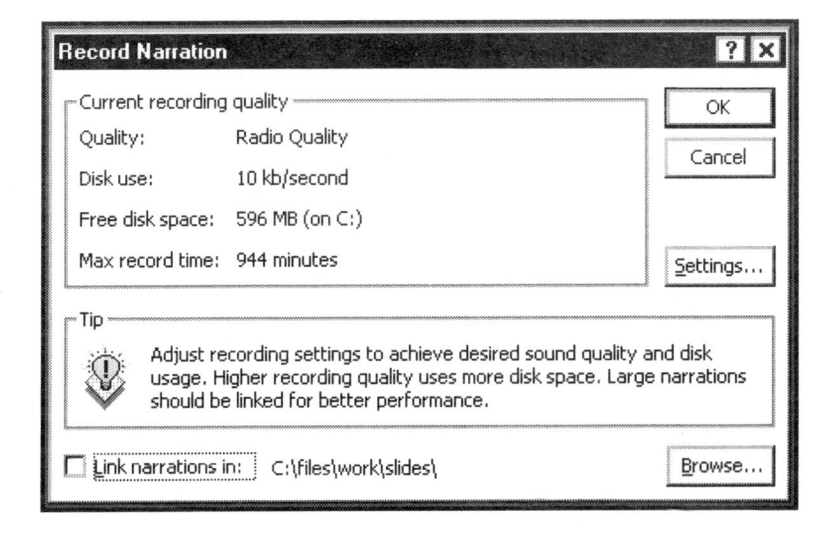

Record Narration		? X
Current recording quality		OK
Quality:	Radio Quality	Cancel
Disk use:	10 kb/second	
Free disk space:	596 MB (on C:)	
Max record time:	944 minutes	Settings...

Tip: Adjust recording settings to achieve desired sound quality and disk usage. Higher recording quality uses more disk space. Large narrations should be linked for better performance.

☐ Link narrations in: C:\files\work\slides\   Browse...

Set Up Show

This option gives you various choices on how you want to run the show.

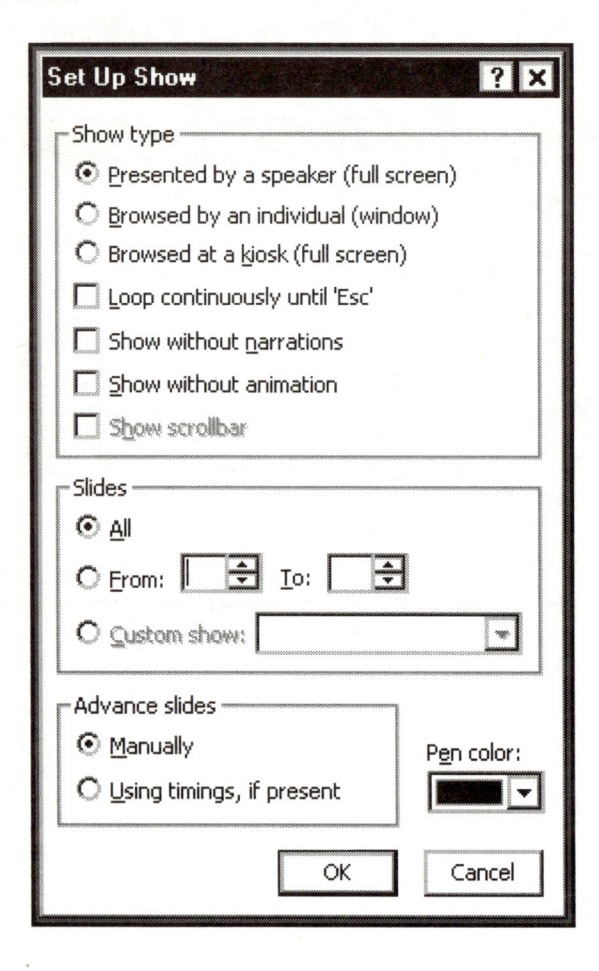

View On Two Screens

You can view your slide show both on your own computer and on an audience computer by using this feature. This may be useful if you do not have access to equipment to project the show onto a larger overhead screen.

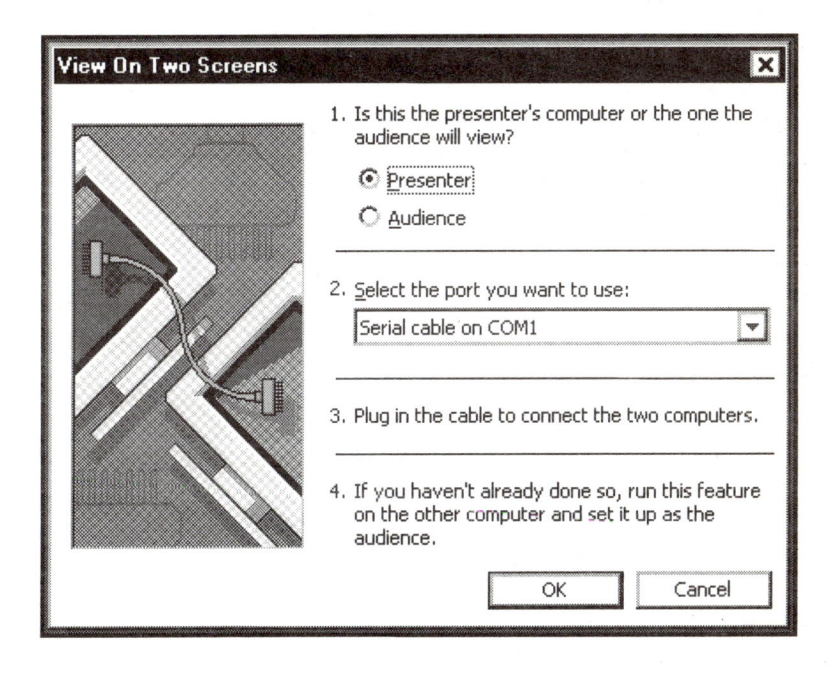

View On Two Screens

1. Is this the presenter's computer or the one the audience will view?
   - ⦿ Presenter
   - ○ Audience

2. Select the port you want to use:
   Serial cable on COM1

3. Plug in the cable to connect the two computers.

4. If you haven't already done so, run this feature on the other computer and set it up as the audience.

   OK   Cancel

Action Buttons

You can add buttons to your slides, which are activated either by clicking the mouse on them or by moving the mouse over them.

You choose your button from the display and then click and drag the mouse to create the button within the slide.

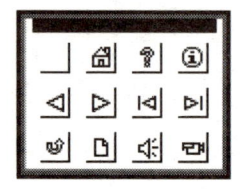

Then you enter the necessary data in the dialog box that will (automatically) appear.

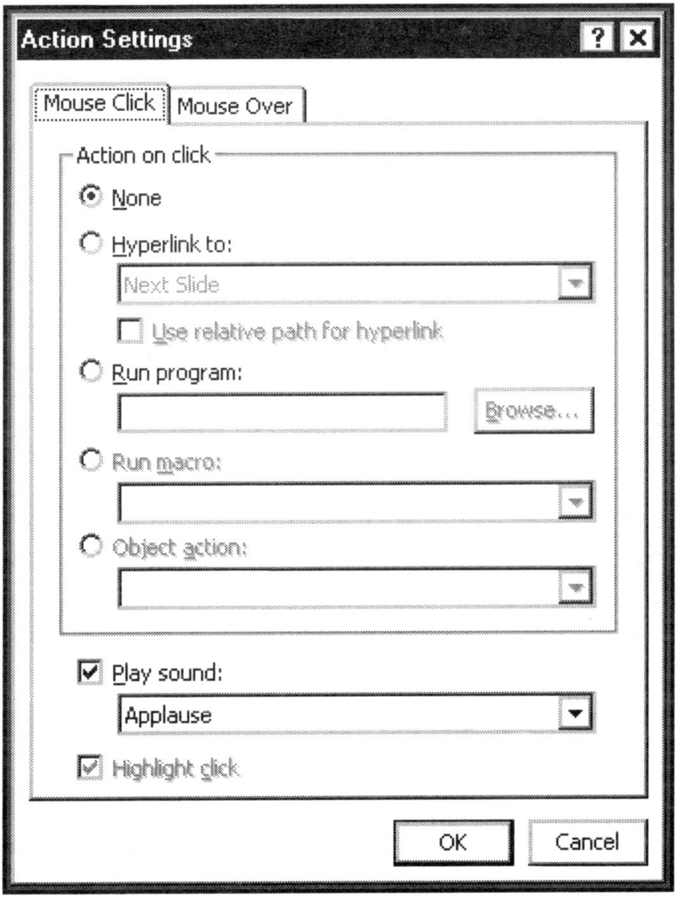
Action Settings
Mouse Click
Mouse Over
Action on click
None
Hyperlink to:
Next Slide
Use relative path for hyperlink
Run program:
Browse...
Run macro:
Object action:
Play sound:
Applause
Highlight click
OK
Cancel

The following illustration shows a sound symbol and I have set the sound to be applause, so whenever I click on the symbol, there will be the sound of applause.

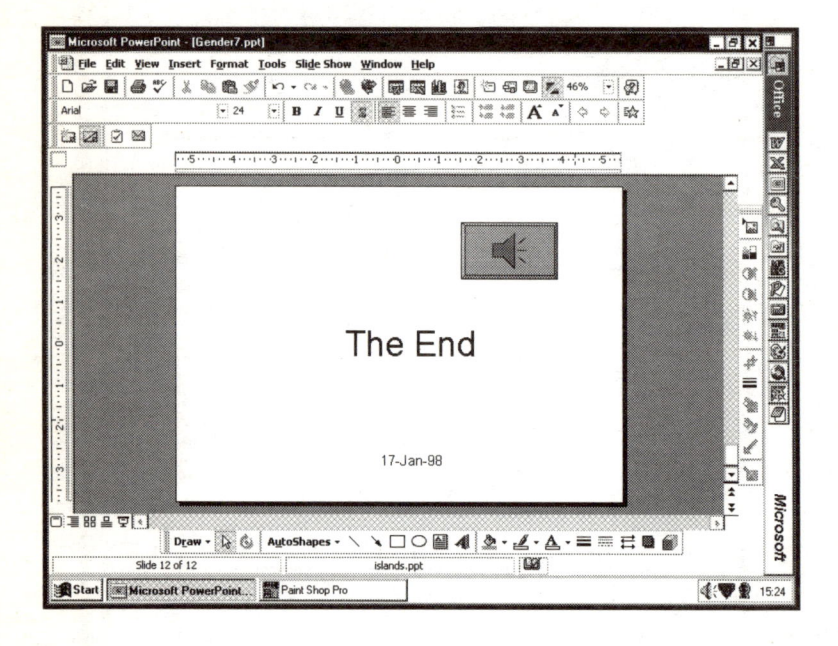

Another use of this technique is to jump to a **Custom Show** (see later) or to another slide show by entering a **Hyperlink to**. This is simply the address of the slide show you want to include (either on the hard disc or on an Intranet or the Internet).

The arrow to the right of the **Hyperlink to** box will give you a choice of places you can jump to.

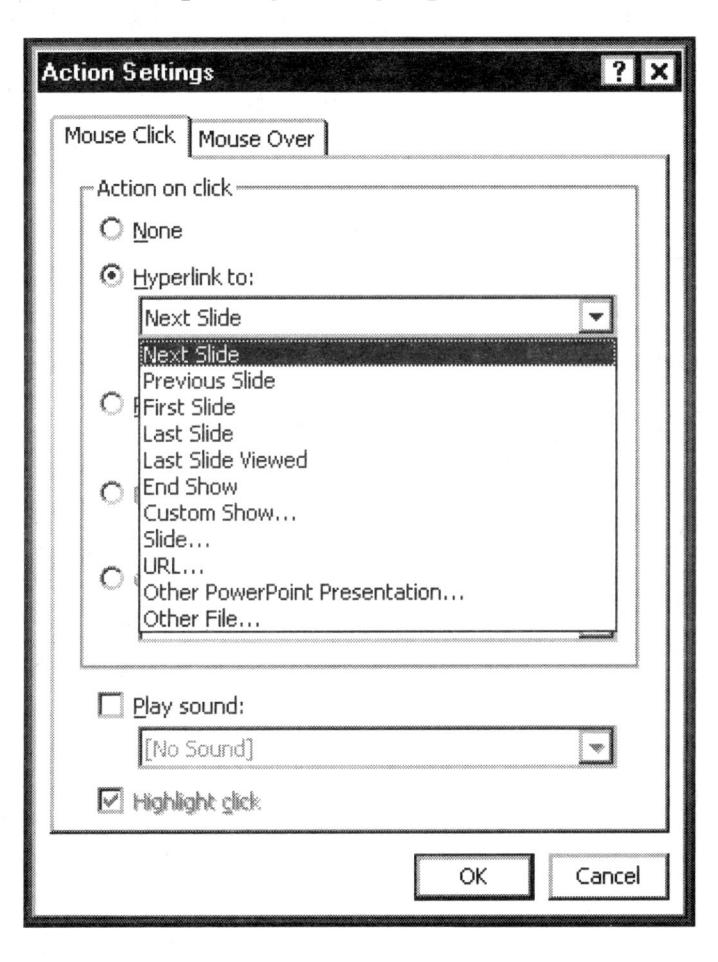

```
Action Settings                                    ? X
┌─────────────┬──────────────┐
│ Mouse Click │ Mouse Over   │
┌─ Action on click ──────────────────────────────┐
│  ○ None                                        │
│                                                │
│  ⊙ Hyperlink to:                               │
│    ┌──────────────────────────────────────┬─┐  │
│    │ Next Slide                           │▼│  │
│    ├──────────────────────────────────────┴─┤  │
│    │ Next Slide                             │  │
│    │ Previous Slide                         │  │
│  ○ │ First Slide                            │  │
│    │ Last Slide                             │  │
│    │ Last Slide Viewed                      │  │
│  ○ │ End Show                               │  │
│    │ Custom Show...                         │  │
│    │ Slide...                               │  │
│    │ URL...                                 │  │
│  ○ │ Other PowerPoint Presentation...       │  │
│    │ Other File...                          │  │
│    └────────────────────────────────────────┘  │
│                                                │
│  □ Play sound:                                 │
│    ┌──────────────────────────────────────┬─┐  │
│    │ [No Sound]                           │▼│  │
│    └──────────────────────────────────────┴─┘  │
│  ☑ Highlight click                             │
└────────────────────────────────────────────────┘
                              ┌────────┐ ┌────────┐
                              │   OK   │ │ Cancel │
                              └────────┘ └────────┘
```

Your choice will determine the next step, for example, if you select **Other PowerPoint Presentation** then a dialog box appears enabling you select the presentation you want to jump to.

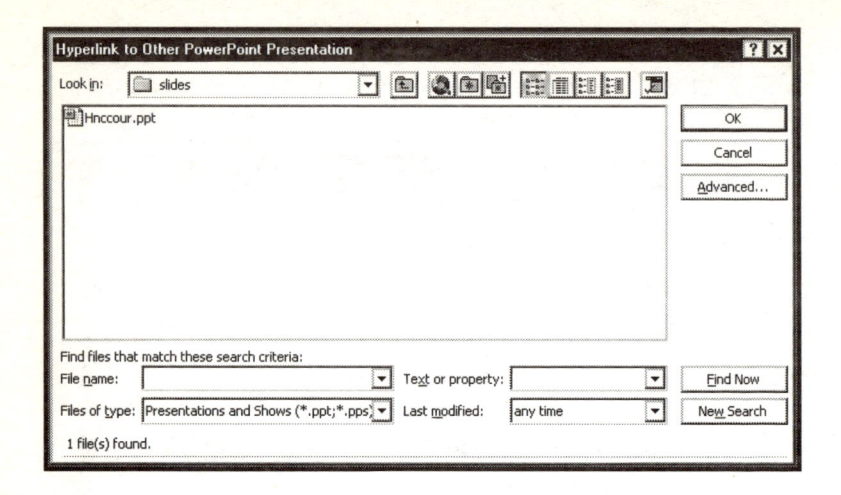

Action Settings

This only becomes available when you have created an action button with settings. You can then alter the settings after selecting the button.

Preset Animation

This gives you a choice of animations (builds) to apply to your slide show. Animation is a special effect that can be applied to text, graphics, buttons, etc. When you run your slide show you will see the animation take place.

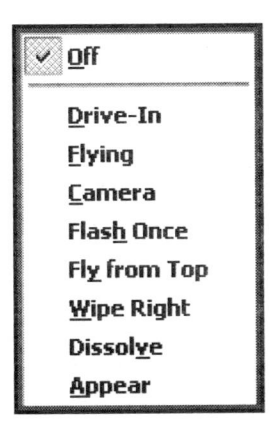

```
✓ Off

  Drive-In
  Flying
  Camera
  Flash Once
  Fly from Top
  Wipe Right
  Dissolve
  Appear
```

If you view the slides in **Slide Sorter View** then you can apply the animation to **all** the contents of all the slides by selecting all the slides (**Edit, Select All**). Alternatively, you can apply the animation to selected slides.

If you view the slides normally, you can select different sections of each slide and apply animation to that section only, e.g. just the text.

Be warned, too many different animations can lead to the viewer paying more attention to the technique and not enough attention to your message.

Custom Animation

This gives you more control over the animations. You can select which parts of the slide to animate, in what order the animations take place, whether the animation is automatic or on a mouse click. You can also alter the **Effects** (the type of animation).

The **Play Settings** option lets you set various features for movie or sound clips you have inserted into the slide show.

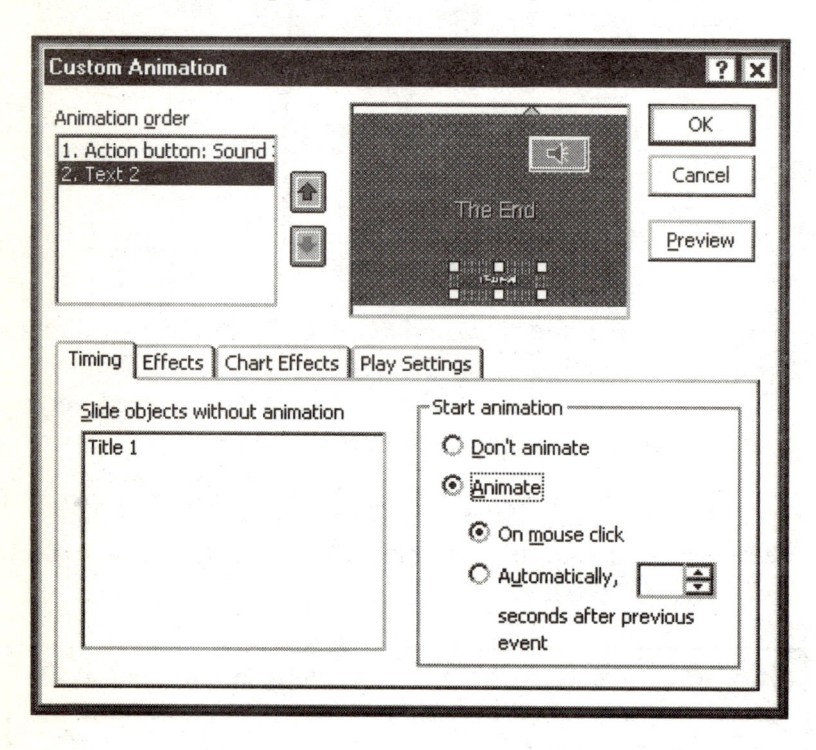

Animation Preview

This previews the animations you have set with a small preview display in the top right corner of the screen.

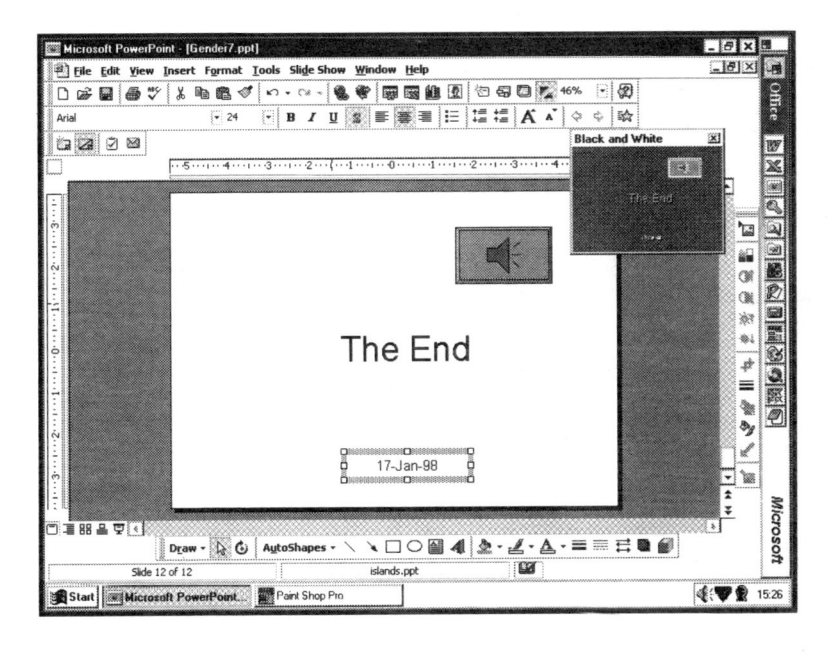

Slide Transition

This is a special effect between each slide, to use this select the **Slide Show** menu and then **Slide Transition**.

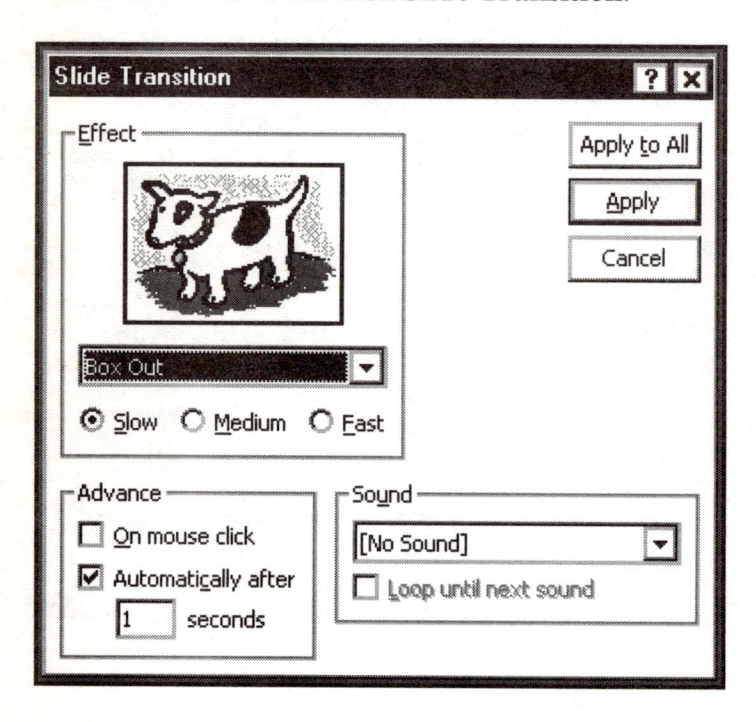

Then select the transition from the (pull down) list and alter the options as you wish. You will see the effect reproduced as you make the changes.

Hide Slide

You can hide slides (within a presentation file) so that they do not display. This may be useful for certain audiences.

You can hide the current slide or if you are in **Slide Sorter View,** you can select several slides.

Remember that if you want to select several slides hold down the **Shift** key while clicking the mouse pointer on each.

To hide a slide use the **Tools** menu and then **Hide Slide**, or if you are in **Slide Sorter View** you can use the **Hide Slide** button (on the upper toolbar).

Displaying Hidden Slides

Type the character **H** while displaying the previous slide.

Alternatively you can click the right hand mouse button and select **Go** from the menu and then **Hidden Slide**.

Custom Shows

You can build up slide shows which contain (some of the) slides from the original slide show. You may want to do this because you are dealing with a variety of audiences, which require a different version of the original. Click on **New** and then you will see the following dialog box.

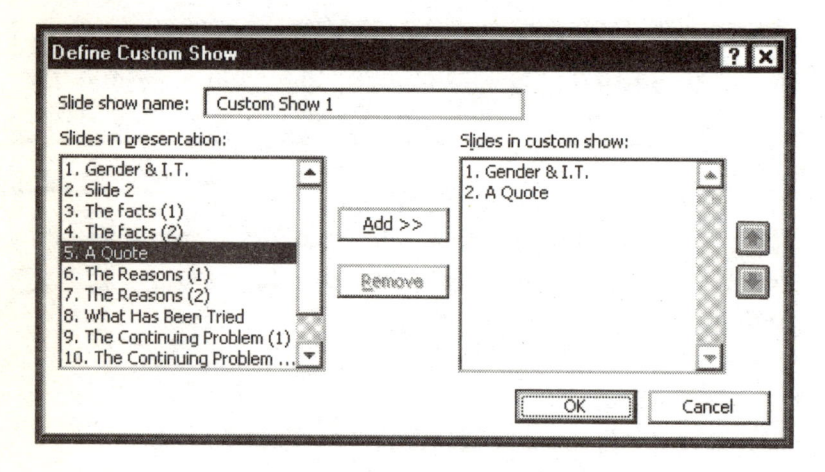

Jumping to other slide shows

If you have a common set of slides and only certain are different for each group then you can jump to a custom show by pulling down the **Slide Show** menu and selecting **Action Settings**, and then setting up a hyperlink to the custom slide show.

Alternatively, you can right-click the mouse and select **Go** on the shortcut menu, then **Custom Show**; finally select the show you want.

The Help menu

As with all Windows programs the on-line **Help** screens are a valuable and easy to use feature of the program and make both learning and problem solving easier.

The Help menu is shown below.

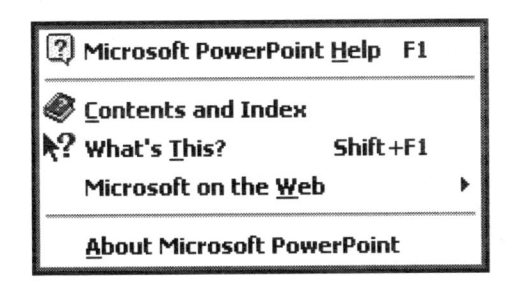

```
[?] Microsoft PowerPoint Help    F1

 🔖 Contents and Index
 ▶? What's This?              Shift+F1
    Microsoft on the Web              ▶

    About Microsoft PowerPoint
```

Contents and Index

You can access Help in three different ways, by using **Contents**, **Index** or **Find**.

Contents

This lists the topics (or books) which contain various hints, tips and explanatory information. Each of these books may contain sections or chapters within it.

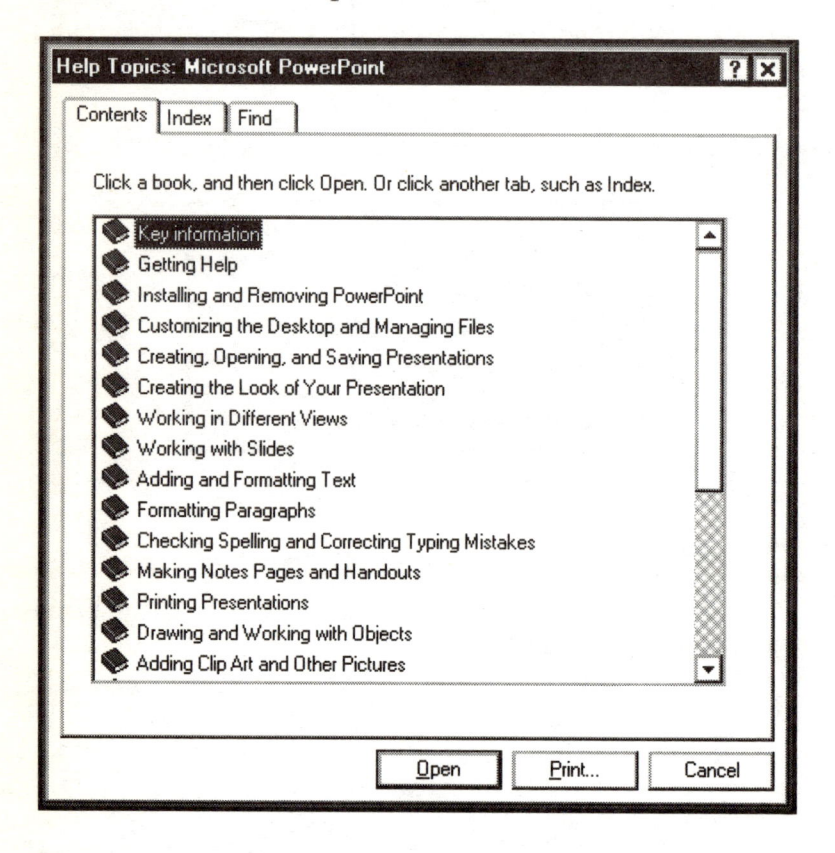

```
Help Topics: Microsoft PowerPoint                    ? X
┌─────────────────────────────────────────────────────┐
│ Contents │ Index │ Find │                           │
└─────────────────────────────────────────────────────┘

  Click a book, and then click Open. Or click another tab, such as Index.

  📚 Key information
  📚 Getting Help
  📚 Installing and Removing PowerPoint
  📚 Customizing the Desktop and Managing Files
  📚 Creating, Opening, and Saving Presentations
  📚 Creating the Look of Your Presentation
  📚 Working in Different Views
  📚 Working with Slides
  📚 Adding and Formatting Text
  📚 Formatting Paragraphs
  📚 Checking Spelling and Correcting Typing Mistakes
  📚 Making Notes Pages and Handouts
  📚 Printing Presentations
  📚 Drawing and Working with Objects
  📚 Adding Clip Art and Other Pictures

              [ Open ]   [ Print... ]   [ Cancel ]
```

You can **Open** any of the books (by clicking on the topic and then on the **Open** button to see the chapters within), for example if you open **Working with Slides** then you can see all the topics under that heading.

Help Topics: Microsoft PowerPoint

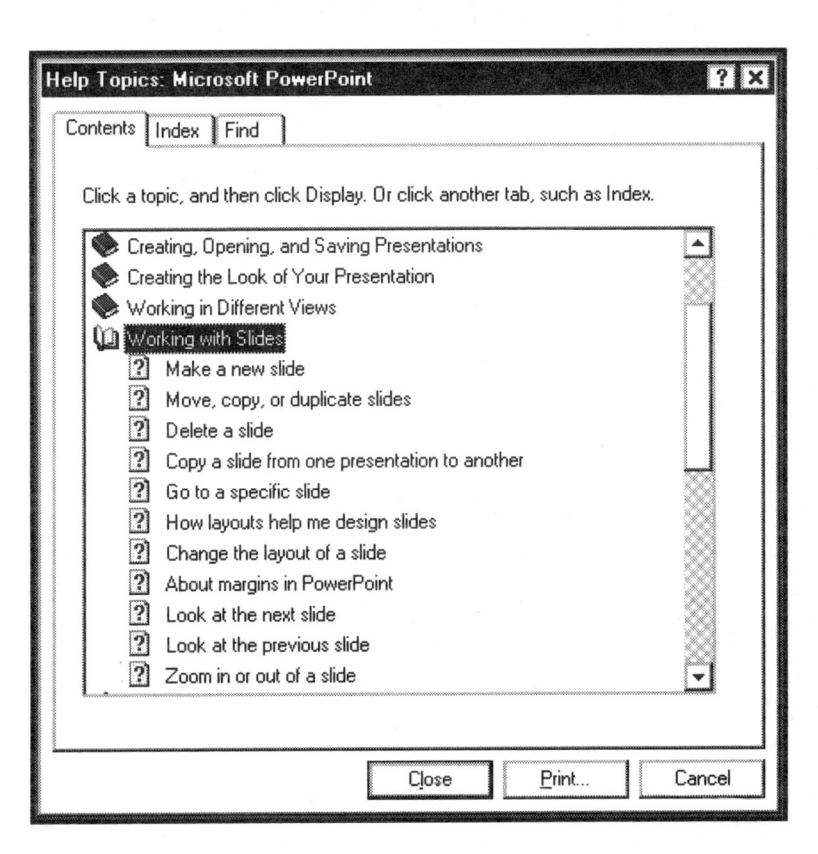

Contents | Index | Find

Click a topic, and then click Display. Or click another tab, such as Index.

- 📚 Creating, Opening, and Saving Presentations
- 📚 Creating the Look of Your Presentation
- 📚 Working in Different Views
- 📖 **Working with Slides**
  - ❓ Make a new slide
  - ❓ Move, copy, or duplicate slides
  - ❓ Delete a slide
  - ❓ Copy a slide from one presentation to another
  - ❓ Go to a specific slide
  - ❓ How layouts help me design slides
  - ❓ Change the layout of a slide
  - ❓ About margins in PowerPoint
  - ❓ Look at the next slide
  - ❓ Look at the previous slide
  - ❓ Zoom in or out of a slide

[Close] [Print...] [Cancel]

Select any of these (by clicking the mouse) and then click on the **Display** button and all will be revealed.

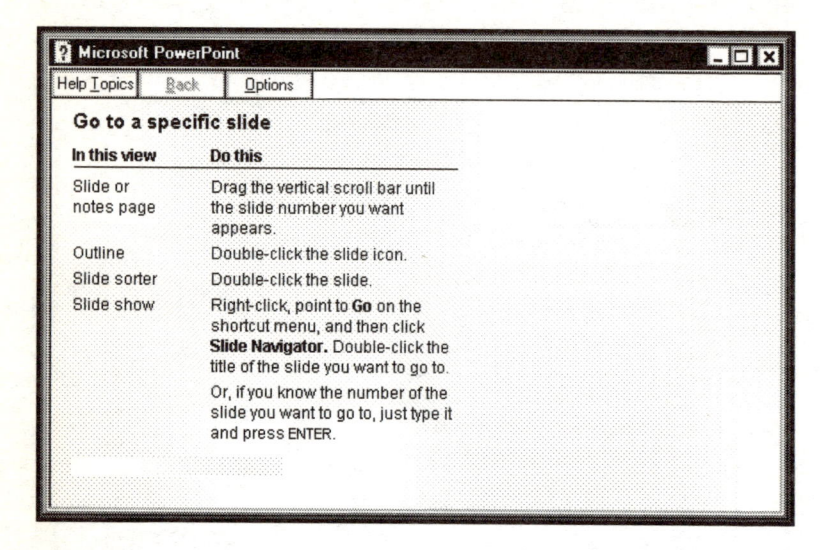

```
Go to a specific slide

In this view      Do this
Slide or          Drag the vertical scroll bar until
notes page        the slide number you want
                  appears.
Outline           Double-click the slide icon.
Slide sorter      Double-click the slide.
Slide show        Right-click, point to Go on the
                  shortcut menu, and then click
                  Slide Navigator. Double-click the
                  title of the slide you want to go to.
                  Or, if you know the number of the
                  slide you want to go to, just type it
                  and press ENTER.
```

You can **Print** the topic instead of reading it on screen; this is useful especially if it is a complex activity.

Links to other Help screens are shown in green type, if you click on them (a hand should appear) you will see another Help screen explaining the relevant topic.

Index

You enter the first few letters of the topic you want to find in the index. If the word or phrase does not exist then the program will find the nearest equivalent (in spelling) to the word you have entered.

Use the scroll bar or cursor keys to move up and down the list.

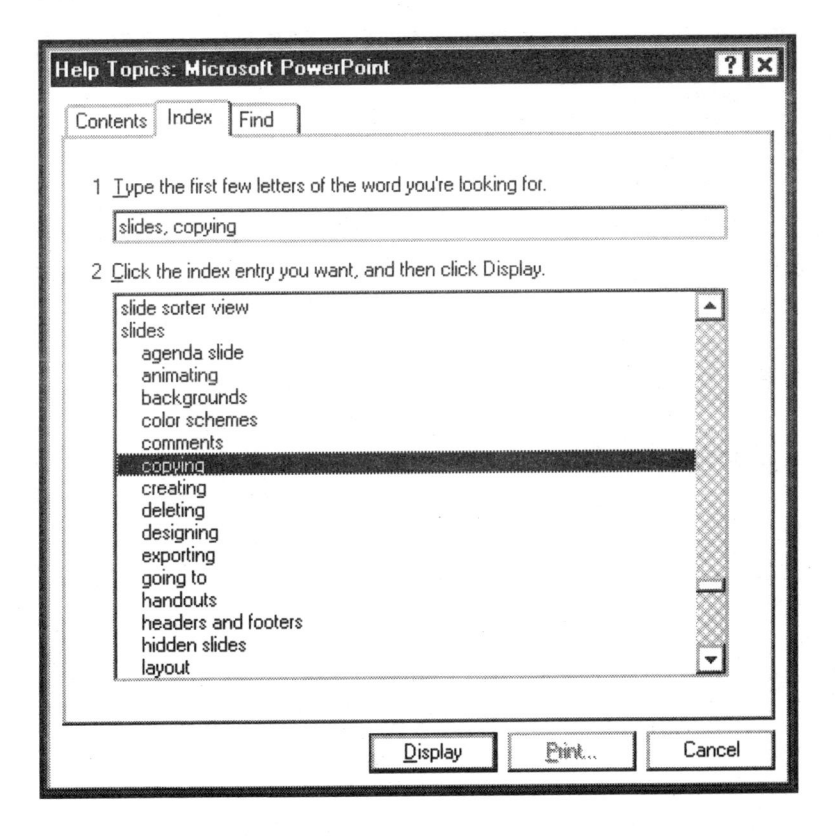

Once you have found the word or phrase you want help on, click the **Display** button to see an explanation of the topic.

Find

The final option within Help is **Find**.

You enter the word or topic you want information on and the program will find it or the nearest equivalent.

The first time you use this, you will have to create a database and you will see the following screen.

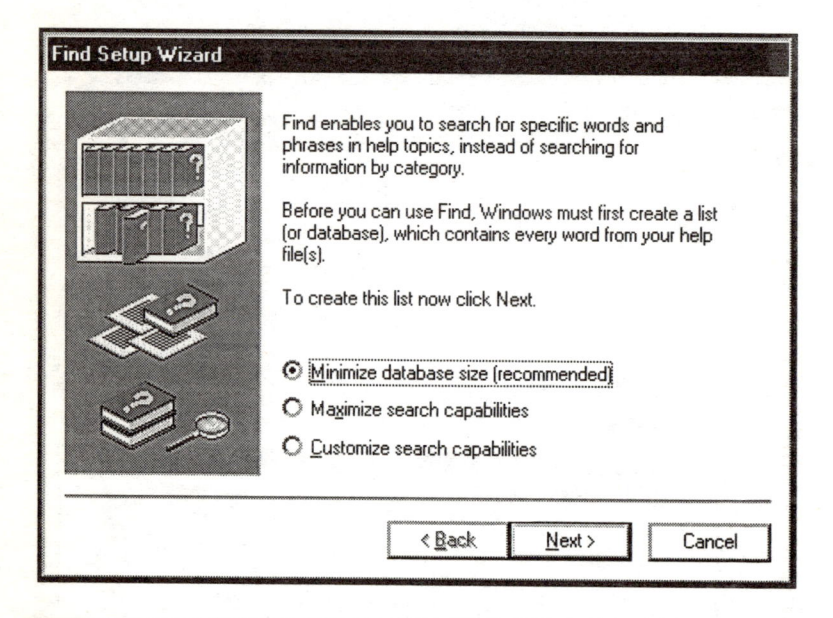

Whichever you choose you can adjust later by selecting the **Rebuild** button in the **Find** dialog box.

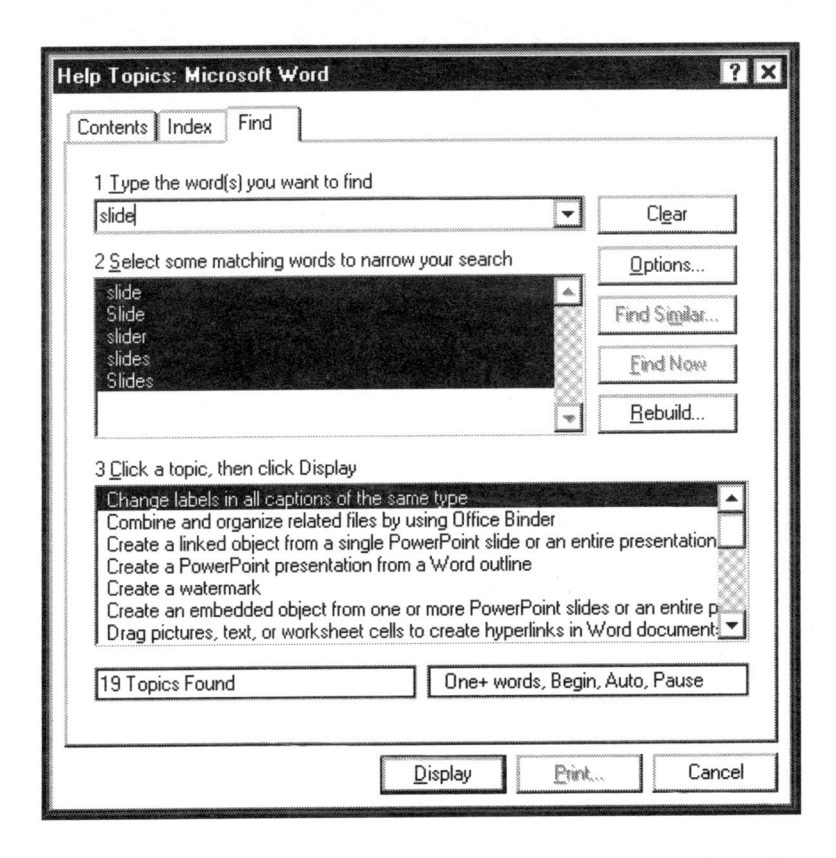

Often you will be presented with a list of items, select the one you want and **Display** the help connected with it.

Note the **Options** button, you can set parameters that are more precise for your search.

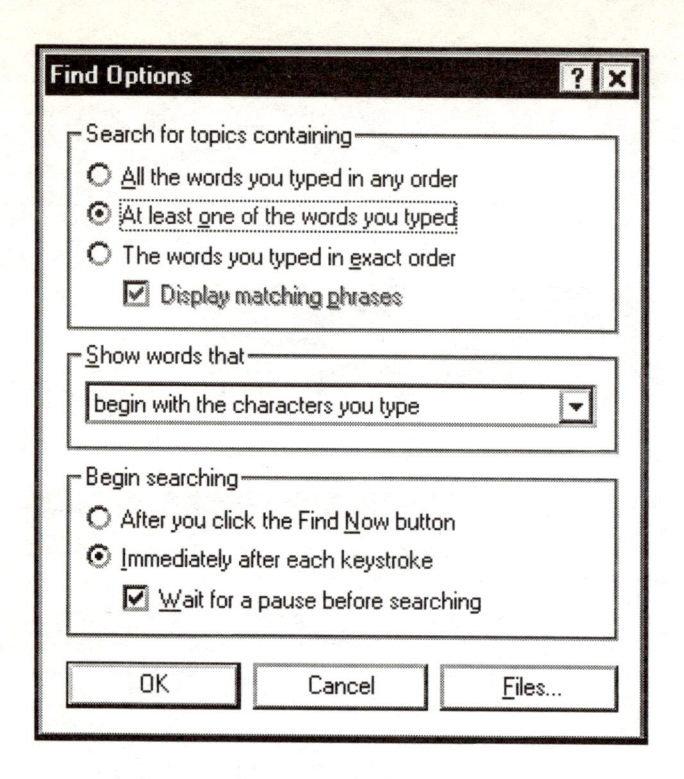

Find is probably the most sophisticated method of accessing information.

The Office Assistant

Do not forget the **Office Assistant** button on the toolbar. This is a quick and easy way of getting help.

An example of what happens when you click on the **Office Assistant** button is shown below.

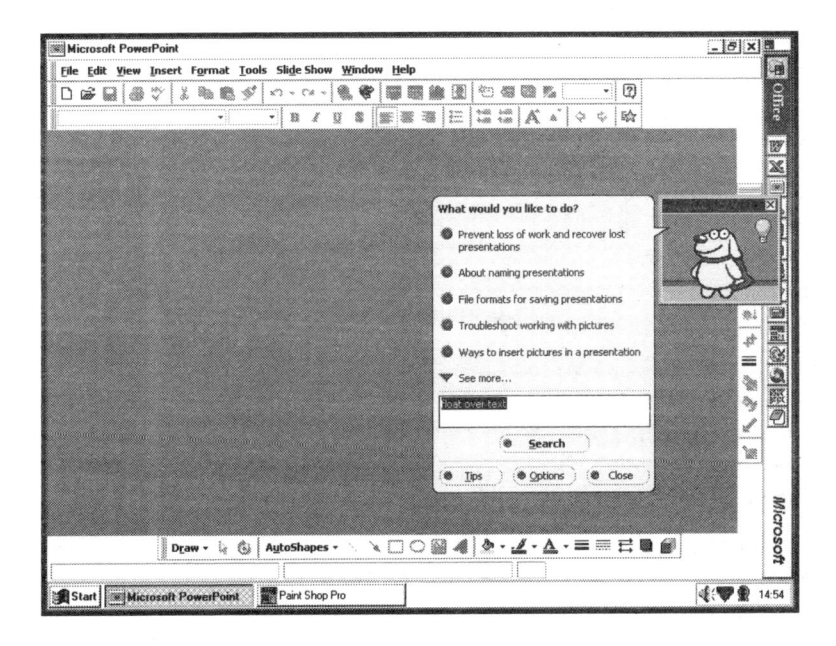

What's This?

Clicking on this displays a tool. You drag this over the problem area and click. You may see an explanation of the topic.

Microsoft on the Web

- **F**ree Stuff
- **P**roduct News
- Frequently Asked **Q**uestions
- Online **S**upport
- Microsoft **O**ffice Home Page
- Send Feedbac**k**...
- **B**est of the Web
- Search the **W**eb...
- Web **T**utorial
- Microsoft **H**ome Page

> To make use of this, you need to be connected to the Internet.

Selecting one of these options will connect you to the relevant Microsoft site on the Internet. Your browser (e.g. Microsoft Explorer) will be loaded and so will the site. An example is shown.

Software Downloads

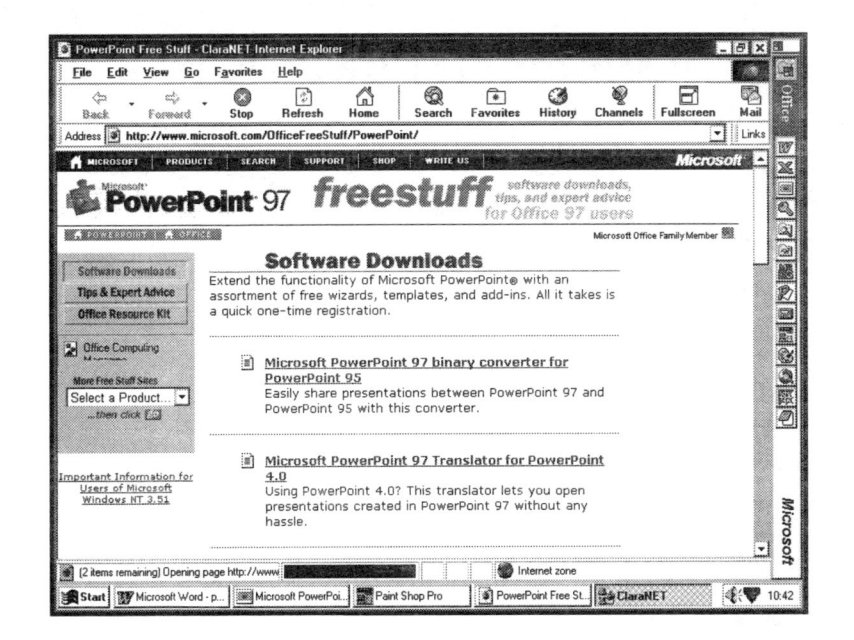

Extend the functionality of Microsoft PowerPoint® with an assortment of free wizards, templates, and add-ins. All it takes is a quick one-time registration.

Microsoft PowerPoint 97 binary converter for PowerPoint 95
Easily share presentations between PowerPoint 97 and PowerPoint 95 with this converter.

Microsoft PowerPoint 97 Translator for PowerPoint 4.0
Using PowerPoint 4.0? This translator lets you open presentations created in PowerPoint 97 without any hassle.

About Microsoft PowerPoint

This displays information about the program.

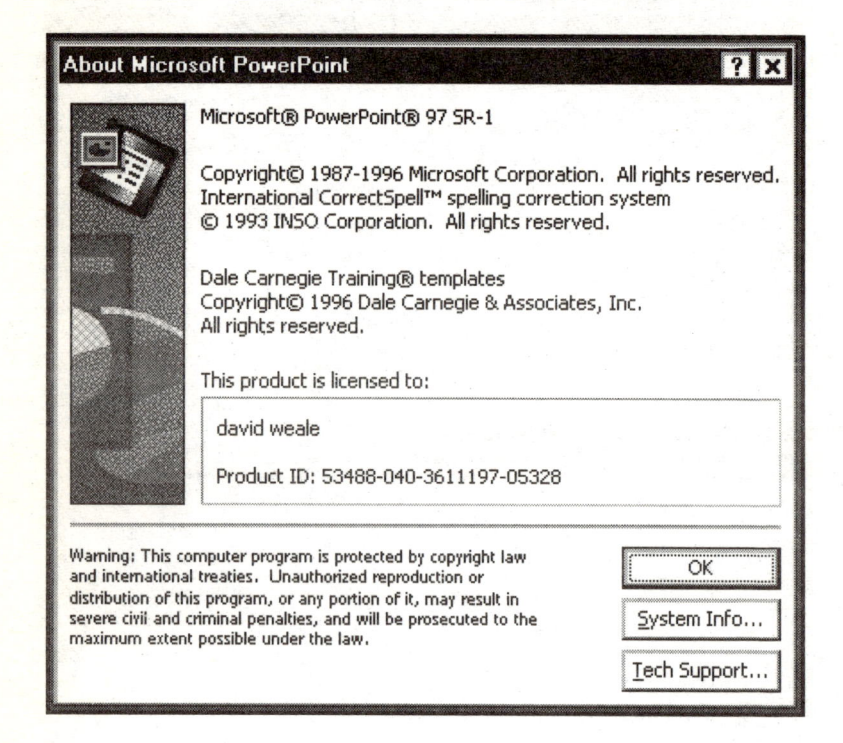

About Microsoft PowerPoint	? X

Microsoft® PowerPoint® 97 SR-1

Copyright© 1987-1996 Microsoft Corporation. All rights reserved.
International CorrectSpell™ spelling correction system
© 1993 INSO Corporation. All rights reserved.

Dale Carnegie Training® templates
Copyright© 1996 Dale Carnegie & Associates, Inc.
All rights reserved.

This product is licensed to:

david weale

Product ID: 53488-040-3611197-05328

Warning: This computer program is protected by copyright law and international treaties. Unauthorized reproduction or distribution of this program, or any portion of it, may result in severe civil and criminal penalties, and will be prosecuted to the maximum extent possible under the law.

OK

System Info...

Tech Support...

If you want to look at **System Info,** you will see a screen similar to this. The screen gives you various data about your system.

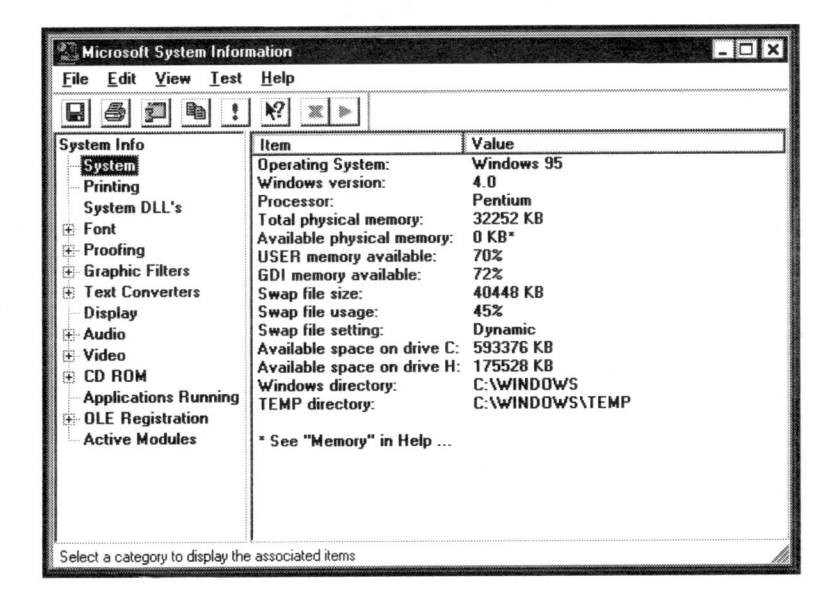

System Info	Item	Value
System	Operating System:	Windows 95
Printing	Windows version:	4.0
System DLL's	Processor:	Pentium
Font	Total physical memory:	32252 KB
Proofing	Available physical memory:	0 KB*
Graphic Filters	USER memory available:	70%
Text Converters	GDI memory available:	72%
Display	Swap file size:	40448 KB
Audio	Swap file usage:	45%
Video	Swap file setting:	Dynamic
CD ROM	Available space on drive C:	593376 KB
Applications Running	Available space on drive H:	175528 KB
OLE Registration	Windows directory:	C:\WINDOWS
Active Modules	TEMP directory:	C:\WINDOWS\TEMP
	* See "Memory" in Help ...	

Select a category to display the associated items

Coping with Presentations

First Things

Decide **WHAT** you want to achieve.

☐ Do you want to impart information or to persuade your audience in some way (e.g. to change their beliefs or attitudes).

☐ Decide upon the type of audience you are addressing and consider what they want from the presentation. Pitch the level of your presentation carefully, audiences vary in their attention span, intellectual ability, etc.

☐ Decide upon the best way to get your message across for the specific audience you are presenting to.

The Material

Write down the main points you want to make and then underneath each main point write the detail. **Outline View** is a very useful tool for this.

The audience likes to have something to take away, so prepare a handout or copy of the OHPs you have used, you can reduce the OHPs so that up to six can be printed onto one page of handout.

The Presentation

Always introduce the material and yourself to the audience and remember to wrap it all up at the end by summarising what you have told them.

Funny (short) stories that are **relevant** help enormously in retaining the audience's attention.

Your voice is of primary importance, keep it slow and interested, emphasise the important points and the changes of topic, this keeps your audience awake.

Always try to maintain eye contact with as many of the audience as possible, this is easiest if you are familiar with your material and do not need to use cue cards to any extent.

Always practise, preferably in front of a live audience or video camera (the first time you see a video of yourself can be traumatic, it is almost as though a stranger is facing you).

The audience is most likely to have a worthwhile experience if you exude enthusiasm, seem to be enjoying yourself and appear to know your subject.

The Environment Itself

Always check the room, seating, lighting and the display equipment (computer, OHP, LCD, etc.) **well before** the actual presentation.

Make sure that all the audience can actually see the screen easily (try not to stand in front of it). Arrange the seating as necessary and adjust any other environmental features (heating, lighting, etc.) to maximise the effect.

Using Software

Keep a consistent style throughout the slides. If you are using Designs, maintain the same one throughout each section of the presentation if not through all of it.

Use clipart, charts or drawings to make points or to amuse but be careful not to detract from the actual message. Using a logo on every slide helps maintain a corporate image. Under no circumstances overdo the use of clipart or other graphics.

Keep the slides as simple as possible, too much detail is pointless and counter-productive, the purpose of the slides is to emphasise the main points of your talk not, usually, to replace the talk itself.

Layout

Use initial capital letters but then lower case (i.e. not all capitals).

Keep the number of words, lines, numbers or graphic images to the absolute minimum for each slide (the maximum number of lines should ideally not be more than six).

Make sensible use of fonts and remember that you need to use large fonts so that the audience can read them easily without effort. It is likely that font sizes less than 18 points will not be readable, in many cases the larger the text the more effective it will be.

You may also like to consider the following:

- Creating a professional finish by ending with a blank coloured slide or a slide with your company logo. This also works well between sections of a presentation

- You can press the **B** character on the keyboard to blank the screen during presentations.

- Use the **Rehearsal** feature to time your slide show (**Slide Show** and then **Rehearse Timings**). As a start, work on the principle that each slide will take around three minutes (although this will vary on the content and how long you talk about it).

Colours and Things

☐ Be careful with your use of colour.

☐ Try to avoid complicated images or backgrounds as these can be confusing to the audience and detract from the points you are trying to put across.

☐ Be aware of contrasts, dark letters on a light backdrop show up well, charts and diagrams also look good with a light (but not too bright) background.

☐ Do not overdo the number or variety of colours or grey shades on any slide and remember that different colours affect the audience in different ways.

Index

A

Action Buttons 152
Add-Ins 142
Alignment 71
Animation 157, 158, 159
Arrows 107
AutoContent 2, 3
AutoShape 73

B

Backgrounds 55, 130, 180
Banner 86
Blank presentation 12
Borders 130
Bring forward 70
Bring to front 70
Browser 79, 82, 84, 86
Build 24
Bullets 123

C

Change case	126
Colour scheme	122
Comments	22, 93, 110, 113
Conference	142
Contents	163, 164
Convert	115
Crop	60
Custom Animation	120, 158
Custom Show	26, 154, 162
Customise	115, 143
Cut	98, 146

D

Date	64
Delete	64, 100
Designs	8, 76, 77, 178
Download	81, 82
Duplicate	100

E

E-mail	82, 92, 93
End Show	29
Environment	178
Equation	39, 57
Excel	39, 43
Explorer	82, 91, 172
Export	27

F

Find 101, 163, 167, 168, 170
Flip 72, 73
Float over Text 132
Font 36, 127
Footer 112
Format painter 134

G

GIF 81
Graph 44, 46
Group 73
Guides 107, 108

H

Handouts 23, 31, 108
Header 112
Help 55, 163
Hidden Slide 26, 161
Hide slide 161
Home page 82
HTML 76, 77, 78, 86
Hyperlink 85, 99, 154, 155, 162

I

Index 163, 167

J

JPEG 81

L

Language 137
Layout 10, 12
Line spacing 124
Links 104

M

Macro 142
Master slide 36, 63, 64, 123
Meeting Minder 27
Move 58, 101
Movie 117, 120, 158

N

Narration 149
Navigator 26
Notes 22, 23

O

Object 39, 58, 60, 73
OHP 23
On-line 76, 77, 78
Options 145
Order 70, 158
Organisation Chart 39, 51, 52, 53, 55, 56
Outlines 4, 17, 23, 114, 115
Outlook 27

P

Pack and Go 89
Paste 98, 99, 146
Paste Special 99
Pen 29
Picture 60, 115, 116
Pngsetup 91
PowerPoint Central 141
Print 23, 30
Profile 92
Properties 96, 102

R

Recolour 67
Regroup 68
Rehearsal 179
Rehearse Timings 148, 179
Replace 101, 127, 146
Resolution 82

Rotate 72, 73
Routing Slip 93

S

Save 32, 33
Scale 31, 115
Scanned images 115
Schedule 27
Select all 52
Send backwards 70
Send To 92
Send to back 70
Sizing 58, 60, 68
Slide Background 130
Slide Layout 10
Slide Meter 28
Slide Miniature 105
Slide Navigator 26
Slide show 7, 22, 23, 24, 179
Slide sorter 6, 20, 64, 100, 114, 161
Smart Quotes 146
Snap to grid 71
Sounds 41, 117, 119, 140
Spelling 38
Statistics 96
Style Checker 136

T

Table 42, 46
Template 8, 11, 12, 36, 122
Text Box 65, 112, 117, 130

Text colour 122
Time 179
Toolbar 1, 32, 56, 143, 144

U

Undo 100
Ungroup 66, 73
Using other computers 89

V

Video 41, 177
View slide 6
Viewer 23, 81, 82, 90, 91, 99, 157

W

Web Page 3, 76, 78, 81, 82, 86
Wizards 4
WordArt 49

Z

Zoom 16, 20